RECONSTRUCTING AMERICA 1865–1890

TEACHING GUIDE
FOR THE REVISED 3RD EDITION

OXFORD

UNIVERSITY PRESS

OXFORD
UNIVERSITY PRESS

Oxford University Press, Inc., publishes works that
further Oxford University's objective of excellence
in research, scholarship, and education.

Oxford New York
Auckland Cape Town Dar es Salaam Hong Kong Karachi
Kuala Lumpur Madrid Melbourne Mexico City Nairobi
New Delhi Shanghai Taipei Toronto

With offices in
Argentina Austria Brazil Chile Czech Republic France Greece
Guatemala Hungary Italy Japan Poland Portugal Singapore
South Korea Switzerland Thailand Turkey Ukraine Vietnam

Writers: Susan Moger, Deborah Parks, Karen Edwards
Editors: Robert Weisser, Susan Moger
Editorial Consultant: Susan Buckley

Published by Oxford University Press, Inc.
198 Madison Avenue, New York, New York, 10016
www.oup.com

Oxford is a registered trademark of Oxford University Press

ISBN-13: 978-0-19-522311-8 (California edition)   ISBN-13: 978-0-19-518892-9

Project Editor: Matt Fisher
Project Director: Jacqueline A. Ball
Education Consultant: Diane L. Brooks, Ed.D.

Casper Grathwohl, Publisher

Printed in the United States
on acid-free paper

CONTENTS

NOTE FROM THE AUTHOR

Dear Teacher,

It is through story that people have traditionally passed on their ideas, their values, and their heritage. In recent years, however, we have come to think of stories as the property of the youngest of our children. How foolish of us. The rejection of story has made history seem dull. It has turned it into a litany of facts and dates. Stories make the past understandable (as well as enjoyable). Stories tell us who we are and where we've been. Without knowledge of our past, we can't make sense of the present.

As a former teacher, I knew of the need for a narrative history for young people, so I sat down and wrote one. (It took me seven years.) I was tired of seeing children struggle with arm-breaking, expensive books. I wanted my books to be inexpensive, light in weight, and user-friendly. Thanks to creative partnering by American Historical Publications and Oxford University Press, that's the way they are.

Called *A History of US*, mine is a set of 11 books. My hope is that they will help make American history—our story—a favorite subject again. It is important that it be so. As we prepare for the 21st century, we are becoming an increasingly diverse people. While we need to celebrate and enjoy that diversity, we also need to find solid ground to stand on together. Our history can provide that commonality. We are a nation built on ideas, on great documents, on individual achievement—and none of that is the property of any one group of us. Harriet Tubman, Abraham Lincoln, Emily Dickinson, Sequoya, and Duke Ellington belong to all of us—and so do our horse thieves, slave owners, and robber barons. We need to consider them all.

Now, to be specific, what do I intend these books to do in your classrooms? First of all, I want to help turn your students into avid readers. I want them to understand that nonfiction can be as exciting as fiction. (Besides, it is the kind of reading they'll meet most in the adult world.) I want to stretch their minds. I've written stories, but the stories are true stories. In nonfiction you grapple with the real world. I want to help children understand how fascinating that process can be.

I've tried to design books that I would have liked as a teacher—books that are flexible, easy-to-read, challenging, and idea-centered, that will lead children into energetic discussions. History can do that. It involves issues we still argue about. It gives us material with which to make judgments. It allows for comparisons. It hones the mind.

People all over this globe are dying—literally—because they want to live under a democracy. We've got the world's model and most of us don't understand or appreciate it. I want to help children learn about their country so they will be intelligent citizens. I want them to understand the heritage that they share with all the diverse people who are us—the citizens of the United States.

For some of your students, these books may be an introduction to history. What they actually remember will be up to you. Books can inspire and excite, but understanding big ideas and remembering details takes some reinforced learning. You'll find many suggestions for that in this Teaching Guide.

What you do with *A History of Us* and this Teaching Guide will depend, of course, on you and your class. You may have students read every chapter or only some chapters, many volumes or only a few. (But, naturally, I hope they'll read it all. Our history makes good reading.) I hope you'll use the books to teach reading and thinking skills as well as history and geography. We need to stop thinking of subjects as separate from each other. We talk about integrating the curriculum; we need to really do it. History, broadly, is the story of a culture—and that embraces art, music, science, mathematics, and literature. (You'll find some of all of those in these books.)

Reading *A History of Us* is easy; even young children seem to enjoy it. But some of the concepts in the books are not easy. They can be challenging to adults, which means that the volumes can be read on several levels. The idea is to get students excited by history and stretched mentally—at whatever their level of understanding. (Don't worry if every student doesn't understand every word. We adults don't expect that of our reading; we should allow for the same variety of comprehension among student readers.)

This Teaching Guide is filled with ideas meant to take the students back to the text to do a careful, searching read. It will also send them out to do research and writing and discovering on their own. The more you involve your students, the more they will understand and retain. Confucius, one of the worlds' great teachers, had this to say:

Tell me and I will forget. Show me and I will remember. Involve me and I will understand.

History is about discovering. It is a voyage that you and your students can embark on together. I wish you good sailing.

Joy Hakim with two of her favorite readers, her grandchildren, Natalie and Sam Johnson

I. STUDENT EDITION

- ► By Joy Hakim, winner of James Michener Prize in Writing
- ► Engaging, friendly narrative
- ► A wide range of primary sources in every chapter
- ► Period illustrations and specially commissioned maps
- ► New atlas section customized for each book

II. TEACHING GUIDE

- ► Standards-based instruction
- ► Wide range of activities and classroom approaches
- ► Strategies for universal access and improving literacy (ELL, struggling readers, advanced learners)
- ► Multiple assessment tools

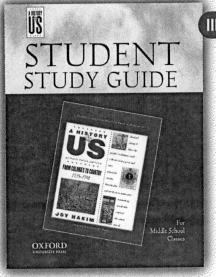

III. STUDENT STUDY GUIDE

- ► Exercises correlated to Student Edition and Teaching Guide
- ► Portfolio approach
- ► Activities for every level of learning
- ► Literacy through reading and writing
- ► Completely new for 2005

SOURCEBOOK AND INDEX

- ► Broad selection of primary sources in each subject area
- ► Ideal resource for in-class exercises and unit projects

Each Teaching Guide is organized into Parts. Each Part includes Chapter Lessons, a Team Learning Project from Johns Hopkins University, Check-up Tests, and other assessments and activities

PARTS
Unify chapter lessons with themes and projects.

INTRODUCTION
▶ Lists standards addressed in each chapter
▶ Gives objectives and big ideas and suggests projects and lessons to set context for the chapters

SUMMARY
▶ Gives assessment ideas and debate, ethics, and interdisciplinary project ideas

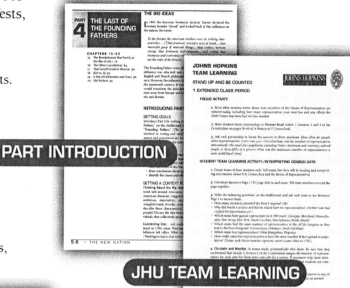

PART INTRODUCTION

JHU TEAM LEARNING

CHAPTER LESSON

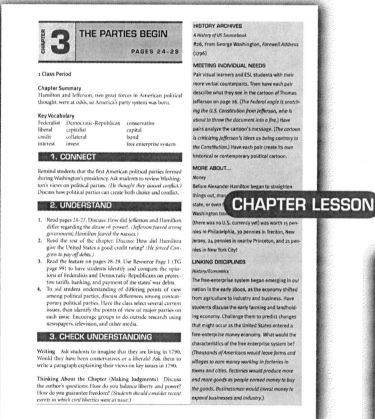

JHU TEAM LEARNING
▶ Each Part contains a cooperative learning project developed by the Talent Development Middle School Program at Johns Hopkins University specifically for *A History of US*.

CHAPTER LESSONS
▶ Correlated to the new Student Study Guide
▶ Ideas for enrichment, discussion, writing, vocabulary, and projects

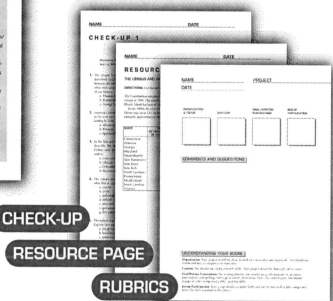

RUBRICS, CHECK-UPS, AND RESOURCE PAGES
▶ Reproduce and hand out for assessment and activities

CHECK-UP

RESOURCE PAGE

RUBRICS

PLANNING LESSONS USING TEACHING AND STUDENT STUDY GUIDES

SET A CONTEXT FOR READING

The books in *A History of US* are written so that a student can read them from cover to cover. You can strengthen students' connection to major themes through introductory lessons or projects. These lessons can be found in the introduction to the Teaching Guide and the opening pages for each Part.

Some students, especially developing readers or those learning English as a second language, may need extra help building background knowledge before reading the text. For these students, exercises in the Teaching and Student Study Guides help to set a context for reading. Look for **Connect** (in the Teaching Guide) and **Access** (in the Student Study Guide) sections. Also, refer to the Improving Literacy section (pages 20–25) for general strategies from an expert.

CREATE A FLEXIBLE CLASSROOM PLAN USING THE STUDENT STUDY GUIDE AND TEACHING GUIDE

The ancillary materials for *A History of US* have been developed for multiple teaching strategies, depending on the particular needs and abilities of your students. Choose an approach that works best for your students. Here are a few options:

▶ **Assign Student Study Guide activities as best suits your class needs**
The Student Study Guide activities are designed to reinforce and clarify content. They were created for students to complete with a minimum of explanation or supervision. The Student Study Guide can be used as homework or in class. The activities can be assigned concurrently with the reading, to help comprehend the material and come to class ready for in-depth discussion of the reading, or as a follow-up to the reading.

▶ **Use Teaching Guide activities to build and enrich comprehension**
The activities from the **Understand** section of each Chapter Lesson, as well as the sidebars, are meant to foster a dynamic, active, vocal classroom. They center on participatory small group and partner projects and focused individual work.

▶ **Use group projects to broaden understanding**
Other suggestions for group projects are found throughout the Teaching Guide, in Part Openers, Part Summaries, and Chapter Lessons. These activities cover a variety of content standard-related topics.

Also, developed specially for *A History of US* are the Johns Hopkins Team Learning Activities, which correlate to Part-wide themes and use cooperative learning models developed by Johns Hopkins University's Talent Development Middle School Program. (For more on these activities and how to use them, see page 21.) Also published by Oxford University Press, a complete curriculum, based on Team Learning Activities for *A History of US* is available. For more information, log on to *www.oup.com*.

Whether projects and assignments are geared toward solidifying understanding of the text or enriching connections with other disciplines is up to you.

▶ **Assign individual work**
Many exercises from the Teaching Guide **Check Understanding** section can be used for individual homework assignments. Student Study Guide pages can be assigned for homework as well.

▶ **Encourage students to create history journals for a portfolio approach**
Student Study Guide pages can be removed from the book and kept in a binder with writing assignments, artwork, and notes from projects as an individual portfolio. This approach creates a history journal, which has many benefits. It can be worked on at home and brought into class for assessment or sharing. It is a student's very own journal, where personal creativity can find an outlet. It also keeps all work organized and in order. Both the Teaching Guide and Student Study Guide contain a variety of analytical and creative writing projects that can be addressed in the history journal.

▶ **Assess however and whenever you need to**
This Teaching Guide contains the following assessment tools: cumulative, synthesis-based project ideas at the end of each Part, wrap-up tests, and scoring rubrics.

RUBRICS
At the back of this Teaching Guide you will find four reproducible rubric pages.

1. The Scoring Rubric page explains the evaluation categories. You may wish to go over and discuss each of these categories and points with your students.

2. A shortened handout version of the Scoring Rubric page has been included, with explanations of the categories and room for comments.

3. A student self-scoring rubric has been included. Use it to prompt your students to describe and evaluate both their work and participation in group projects.

4. A library/media center research log has also been included. Use this rubric as an aid to student research. It will help them plan and brainstorm research methods, record results, and evaluate their sources.

ASSESSMENT OPPORTUNITIES
Part Summaries were written specifically to give assessment ideas. They do this in two ways:

1. They refer to Part Check-Ups—reproducible tests at the back of the Teaching Guide that combine multiple choice, short answer, and an essay question to present a comprehensive assessment that covers the chapters in each Part.

2. They contains additional essay questions for alternate assessment as well as numerous project ideas. Projects can be assessed using the scoring rubrics at the back of the Teaching Guide.

ANSWER KEYS
An answer key at the back of the Teaching Guide contains answers for Part Check-Ups, Resource Pages, and Student Study Guide activities.

The Student Study Guide complements the activities in the Teaching Guide with exercises that build a context for the reading and strengthen analysis skills. Many activities encourage informal small group or family participation. In addition, the following features make it an effective teaching tool:

FLEXIBILITY

You can use the Study Guide in the classroom, with individuals or small groups, or send it home for homework. You can distribute the entire guide to students; however, the pages are perforated so you can remove and distribute only the pertinent lessons.

A page on reports and special projects in the front of the Study Guide directs students to the "More Books to Read" resource in the student edition. This feature gives students general guidance on doing research and devising independent study projects of their own.

FACSIMILE SPREAD

The Study Guide begins with a facsimile spread from the Student Edition. This spread gives reading strategies and highlights key features: captions, primary sources, sidebars, headings, etymologies. The spread supplies the contextualization students need to fully understand the material.

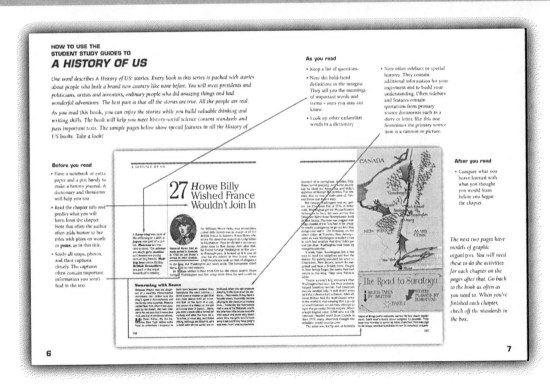

PORTFOLIO APPROACH

The Study Guide pages are three-hole-punched so they can be integrated with notebook paper in a looseleaf binder. This history journal or portfolio can become both a record of content mastery and an outlet for each student's unique creative expression. Responding to prompts, students can write poetry or songs, plays and character sketches, create storyboards or cartoons, or construct multi-layered timelines.

The portfolio approach gives students unlimited opportunities for practice in areas that need strengthening. And the Study Guide pages in the portfolio make a valuable assessment tool for you. It is an ongoing record of performance that can be reviewed and graded periodically.

GRAPHIC ORGANIZERS

This feature contains reduced models of seven graphic organizers referenced frequently in the guide. Using these devices will help students organize the material so it is more accessible. (Full-size reproducibles of each graphic organizer are provided at the back of this Teaching Guide.) These graphic organizers include: outline, main idea map, K-W-L chart (What I Know, What I Want to Know, What I Learned), Venn diagram, timeline, sequence of events chart, and t-chart.

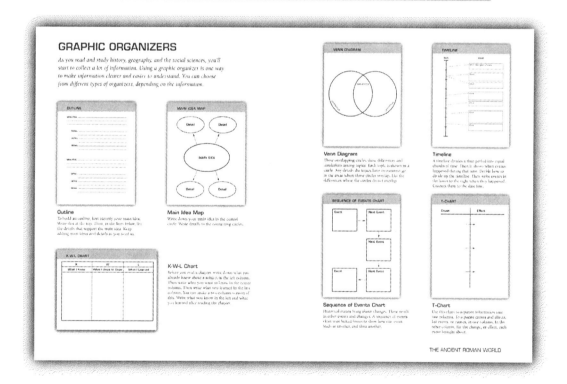

Each chapter lesson is designed to draw students into the subject matter. Recurring features and exercises challenge their knowledge and allow them to practice valuable analysis skills. Activities in the Teaching Guide and Student Study Guide complement but do not duplicate each other. Together they offer a wide range of class work, group projects, and opportunities for further study and assessment that can be tailored to all ability levels.

CHAPTER SUMMARY
briefly reviews big ideas from the chapter.

ACCESS
makes content accessible to students of all levels by incorporating graphic organizers into note taking.

WRITING
gives students writing suggestions drawn from the material. A writing assignment may stem from a vocabulary word, a historical event, a person, or a reading of a primary source. The assignment can take any number of forms: newspaper article, letter, short essay, a scene with dialogue, a diary entry.

CHAPTER 2 — ABOUT BEING A PRESIDENT

SUMMARY *George Washington chose advisers to help him run the country.*

ACCESS

Have you ever tried to do a really hard job by yourself? Hard jobs are usually easier when you get people to help. President Washington could not run the country by himself. He needed advisers to assist him. Copy the main idea map from page 8 into your history journal. In the largest circle, put Washington's name. In each of the smaller circles, write the name of one of the people who helped Washington govern the nation. Below each name, write the job that the person had.

WORD BANK   precedent   executive   legislative   judicial   cabinet   dictatorship

Choose words from the word bank to complete the sentences. One word is not used at all.

1. The _____ branch includes the nation's courts.

2. A government that is run by an all-powerful leader is called a _____.

3. The president is the head of the _____ branch.

4. Washington chose Henry Knox to serve in his _____.

5. Congress is also called the _____ branch.

WORD PLAY

In the dictionary, look up the word you did not use. Write a sentence using that word.

_____

WITH A PARENT OR PARTNER

The United States has a three-branch government. Write the name of each branch at the top of a piece of paper. Below each name, write five words that relate to that particular branch of government. Ask a parent or partner to do the same. Then read your lists to each other.

WORKING WITH PRIMARY SOURCES

In 1792 Dr. Benjamin Rush wrote this about a hot air balloon flight by Jean-Pierre François Blanchard:

> For some time days past the conversation in our city has turned wholly upon Mr. Blanchard's late Aerial Voyage. It was truly a sublime sight. Every faculty of the mind was seized, expanded and captivated by it, 40,000 people concentrating their eyes and thoughts at the same instant, upon the same object, and all deriving nearly the same degree of pleasure from it.

1. How did Benjamin Rush feel about Blanchard's flight?

2. How did the people of Philadelphia feel about Blanchard's flight?

WRITING

Imagine that you are in Philadelphia watching Blanchard's flight. In your history journal, write a letter to a friend describing the event in your own words.

12   CHAPTER 2

Tap Prior Knowledge

What students know about the topic will help determine your next steps for instruction. Using K-W-L charts, brainstorming, and making lists are ways to find out what they know. English learners bring a rich cultural diversity into the classroom. By sharing what they know, students can connect their knowledge and experiences to the course.

Set the Context

Use different tools to make new information understandable. These can be images, artifacts, maps, timelines, illustrations, charts, videos, or graphic organizers. Techniques such as role-playing and storyboarding can also be helpful. Speak in shorter sentences, with careful enunciation, expanded explanations, repetitions, and paraphrasing. Use fewer idiomatic expressions.

Show—Don't Just Tell

English learners often get lost as they listen to directions, explanations, lectures, and discussions. By showing students what is expected, you can help them participate more fully in classroom activities. Students need to be shown how to use the graphic organizers in the student study guide, as well as other blackline masters for note-taking and practice. An overhead transparency with whole or small groups is also effective.

Use the Text

Because of unfamiliar words, students will need help with understanding. Teach them to preview the chapter using text features (headings, bold print, sidebars, italics). See the suggestions in the facsimile of the Student Edition, shown on pages 6–7 of the Student Study Guide. Show students organizing structures such as cause and effect or comparing and contrasting. Have students read to each other in pairs. Help them create word banks, charts, and graphic organizers. Discuss the main idea after reading.

Check for Understanding

Rather than simply ask students if they understand, stop frequently and ask them to paraphrase or expand on what you just said. Such techniques will give you a much clearer assessment of their understanding.

Provide for Interaction

As students interact with the information and speak their thoughts, their content knowledge and academic language skills improve. Increase interaction in the classroom through cooperative learning, small group work, and partner share. By working and talking with others, students can practice asking and answering questions.

Use Appropriate Assessment

When modifying the instruction, you will also need to modify the assessment. Multiple choice, true and false, and other criterion reference tests are suitable, but consider changing test format and structure. English learners are constantly improving their language proficiency in their oral and written responses, but they are often grammatically incorrect. Remember to be thoughtful and fair about giving students credit for their content knowledge and use of academic language, even if their English isn't perfect.

STRUGGLING READERS

Some students struggle to understand the information presented in a textbook. The following strategies for content-area reading can help students improve their ability to make comparisons, sequence events, determine importance, summarize, evaluate, synthesize, analyze, and solve problems.

Build Knowledge of Genre

Both fiction and narrative nonfiction genres are incorporated into *A History of US*. This combination of genres makes the text interesting and engaging. But teachers must be sure students can identify and use the organizational structures of both genres.

The textbook has a wealth of the text features of nonfiction: bold and italic print, sidebars, headings and subheadings, labels, captions, and "signal words" such as first, next, and finally. Teaching these organizational structures and text features is essential for struggling readers.

Fiction

Each chapter is a story

Setting: historical time and place

Characters: historical figures

Plot: problems, roadblocks, and resolutions

Non-Fiction

Content: historical information

Organizational structure: cause/effect, sequence of events, problem/solution

Other features: maps, timelines, sidebars, photographs, primary sources

Build Background

Having background information about a topic makes reading about it so much easier. When students lack background information, teachers can preteach or "front load" concepts and vocabulary, using a variety of instructional techniques. Conduct a "chapter or bookwalk," looking at titles, headings, and other text features to develop a big picture of the content. Focus in new vocabulary words during the "walk" and create a word bank with illustrations for future reference. Read aloud key passages and discuss the meaning. Focus on the timeline and maps to help students develop a sense of time and place. Show a video, go to a website, and have trade books and magazines on the topic available for student exploration.

Comprehension Strategies

While reading, successful readers are predicting, making connections, monitoring, visualizing, questioning, inferring, and summarizing. Struggling readers have a harder time with these "in the head" processes. The following strategies will help these students construct meaning from the text until they are able to do it on their own.

Predict

Before reading, conduct a picture and text feature "tour" of the chapter to make predictions. Ask students if they remember if this has ever happened before, to predict what might happen this time.

Make Connections

Help students relate content to their background (text to text, text to self, and text to the world).

Monitor And Confirm

Encourage students to stop reading when they come across an unknown word, phrase, or concept. In their notebooks, have them make a note of text they don't understand and ask for clarification or figure it out. While this activity slows down reading at first, it is effective in improving skills over time.

Visualize

Students benefit from imagining the events described in a story. Sketching scenes, story-boarding, role-playing, and looking for sensory details all help students with this strategy.

Infer

Help students look beyond the literal meaning of a text to understand deeper meanings. Graphic organizers and discussions provide opportunities to broaden their understanding. Looking closely at the "why" of historical events helps students infer.

Question And Discuss

Have students jot down their questions as they read, and then share them during discussions. Or have students come up with the type of questions they think a teacher would ask. Over time students will develop more complex inferential questions, which lead to group discussions. Questioning and discussing also helps students see ideas from multiple perspectives and draw conclusions, both critical skills for understanding history.

Determine Importance

Teach students how to decide what is most important from all the facts and details in non-fiction. After reading for an overall understanding, they can go back to highlight important ideas, words, and phrases. Clues for determining importance include bold or italic print, signal words, and other text features. A graphic organizer such as a main idea map also helps.

Teach and Practice Decoding Strategies

Rather than simply defining an unfamiliar word, teach struggling readers decoding strategies: have them look at the prefix, suffix, and root to help figure out the new word, look for words they know within the word, use the context for clues, and read further or reread.

— *Cheryl A. Caldera, M.A.*
Literacy Coach

TEACHING STRATEGIES FOR *RECONSTRUCTING AMERICA*

INTRODUCING BOOK SEVEN

All persons born or naturalized in the United States, and subject to the jurisdiction thereof, are citizens of the United States and of the State wherein they reside. No State shall make or enforce any law which shall abridge the privileges or immunities of citizens of the United States; nor shall any State deprive any person of life, liberty, or property, without due process of law; nor deny to any person within its jurisdiction the equal protection of the laws.

—The Constitution of the United States, 14th Amendment, Section 1

HISTORICAL OVERVIEW

Cartoon about impeachment of President Johnson

Adopted in 1868, the 14th Amendment symbolized the best of Reconstruction—the urge to extend justice to all Americans. But passage of the Amendment did not come without a fight. President Andrew Johnson attacked it; twelve southern and border states rejected it. Resistance to the 14th Amendment handed control of Reconstruction to the Radical Republicans. Firebrands such as Thaddeus Stephens in the House and Charles Sumner in the Senate vowed to reshape southern society. In 1867, federal troops marched into the South and initiated Military Reconstruction. For southern states, the price of readmission to the Union became ratification of the 14th Amendment.

In 1869, in a further effort to write democratic principles and color blindness into the Constitution, the Radicals succeeded in pushing through the 15th Amendment for ratification. This measure forbade states to deny the right to vote "on account of race, color, or previous condition of servitude." Armed with the vote and backed by federal troops, African Americans won election to political offices at the local, state, and national levels for the first time in the nation's history. But their victories proved short-lived.

The moral fervor of the war and the passions of Reconstruction left the nation exhausted. When the southern states completed their march back into the Union, the North turned its attention to other matters. Amid the fury of a white backlash, African Americans found themselves the target of pent-up anger over Military Reconstruction. Therefore, although Reconstruction had proclaimed anew the American principle of human equality, it failed to secure it in reality. The South fell back into the hands of white Southerners and a new racial tyranny named Jim Crow.

On the cattle drive

In the closing years of the century, the pace of life quickened. Pioneers spilled pell-mell across the Mississippi. Cattle kings and sodbusters battled Native Americans for their last homeland. Railroad crews blasted through mountains and laid track across the Plains. Meanwhile, immigrants poured into the United States by the millions. In assessing the period, economist and social reformer Henry George remarked:

There is in all the past nothing to compare with the rapid changes now going on.... The snail's pace of crawling ages has suddenly become the headlong rush of the locomotive.

When the United States celebrated its one-hundredth birthday in 1876, most Americans welcomed the chance to focus on

Shooting buffalo from a train

Sitting Bull, Sioux chief

Susan B. Anthony surrounded by other founders of NAWSA

Family in tenement apartment

the marvels of progress rather than the agonies of Reconstruction. They celebrated American inventiveness in a grand Centennial Exposition held in Philadelphia. For six months, some 10 million people strolled through Machinery Hall to glimpse the start of the industrial age. But the Centennial Exposition showed only one side of American life. It concealed the unresolved issue of equality. The sight of Susan B. Anthony reading the Declaration of Sentiments at the Woman's Building hinted at the lack of rights for women. But few people paid any attention to Anthony—women's suffrage belonged to the next century. Even less attention was paid to the lack of rights for Native Americans and the African Americans who staggered under the heavy hand of the institutionalized segregation called Jim Crow. The glaring gaps between the rich and poor were also absent from the fair. Most of the poor could barely afford to eat, much less buy a ticket to attend the Exposition.

The growing pains of rapid change could be felt all across the continent—in the West where Native Americans lost their land, on the Pacific Coast where Asian immigrants felt the sting of prejudice, in the South where blacks and whites tried to build a "New South," in the East and Midwest where immigrants swelled the cities and fueled new industries with their labor. Guiding the nation through this period of turmoil were the same principles that had guided it through the trauma of its revolutionary birth. Americans still clung to the ideals proclaimed by the Declaration of Independence. So did the millions of immigrants who came to the United States in pursuit of these ideals. It was these beliefs that united the nation's diverse people and directed their search for perfection. Declared civil rights defender W. E. B. DuBois:

We are Americans, not only by birth and by citizenship, but by our political ideals....And the greatest of those ideals is that ALL MEN [AND WOMEN] ARE CREATED EQUAL.

Book Seven traces the passage of the United States into the modern era and its second century of existence as a "government of the people, by the people, and for the people." Each of the seven parts, or units of study, serves as a "road marker" on the journey.

INTRODUCING THE BIG IDEAS

Reconstructing America (Book Seven in *A History of US*) explores three Big Ideas: **change**, **justice**, and **diversity**. Introducing your students to these concepts at the beginning will help them put together the pieces of the puzzle to make sense of the past. One starting point might be to write the title of this book on the chalkboard—*Reconstructing America*. Pointing out that the prefix *re-* means "again" or "anew," help students decode the key word in the title: *re-constructing = re-building = re-shaping*. Discuss the implications of change in this word.

Now challenge students to think of ways America needed rebuilding in the years following the Civil War. (You may want students to "re-view" the closing chapters in Book Six.) Lead students to understand that the nation still had to grapple with extending justice to those who had been enslaved. It also had to find a just policy for dealing with the South.

To introduce the concept of diversity, have students move past the title and into the Table of Contents. Ask them which chapter titles show that the United States was becoming more diverse geographically. Which titles show that it was becoming more diverse culturally? You might link the concepts of diversity and justice by asking students to consider what might happen to the United States if equal justice were not extended to all its diverse peoples. Would the democracy continue to work? Why or why not?

FOCUSING ON LITERACY

SETTING THE CONTEXT

You might set the stage for Book Seven by reading aloud the selection from the 14th Amendment on TG page 12. Your students may have read about the 14th Amendment in Book Six, but tell them that the story of the 14th Amendment isn't finished. In fact, its story runs all through Book Seven. Then read aloud the title of Part 7 in Book Seven. Do students think the story of the 14th Amendment is concluded in this book? Why or why not? *(No, because the title of Part 7 is "The Unfinished Journey.")*

To set the stage for Book Seven and the ongoing search for justice, have students read the Preface on pages 9-11. Be prepared for some debate. The Preface asks students to think ethically about some controversial issues such as capital punishment and abortion. Although you won't resolve these issues in class, you may want to allow students to argue about them. Use the arguments to show that the debate over the meaning of justice—i.e., the 14th Amendment's "due process of law"—is still going on in the present.

ANALYZING CHARACTER

In every era, the character of leaders affects the outcome of history, but for the era covered in Book Seven, a study of character brings into focus some of the reasons why Reconstruction was a failed Revolution and what the abiding consequences of that failure were. The characters of President Johnson and Thaddeus Stevens, as well as other members of Congress from North and South,

INTRODUCING THE BOOK WITH PROJECTS AND ACTIVITIES

determined how the peace was conducted. Discuss the terms "character" and "good character" with students to understand what the terms mean to them. Invite students to analyze the character of key figures as they read Book Seven. Influential Americans such as Chief Joseph, W. E. B. DuBois, Susan B. Anthony, Ida B. Wells, and Thomas Edison inspired people of their time and people today. As in all volumes of *A History of US*, the character of the American people during the era is explored in Book Seven.

READING FURTHER

The era covered in Book Seven has its share of wonderful reading for students and teachers. Locate copies of a book of Edward Curtis photographs of Native Americans (there is a paperback version) and Frederick Remington's paintings of a vanished West. Read Mark Twain aloud. Encourage students to bring in books on cowboys, inventors, scientists, and Native American and African American leaders. They can also draw on a wealth of material by and about nineteenth-century women—from biographies of women who fought for causes such as civil rights for African Americans and women's suffrage to fiction, diaries, and photographic collections documenting the experience of homesteading on the Great Plains.

ONGOING PROJECTS

The following activities bridge the seven parts in *Reconstructing America*.

USING TIME LINES

Author Joy Hakim advises that a sense of chronology—rather than memorized dates—is what matters for students. Various kinds of time lines are invaluable aids in building this understanding of historical sequence.

Book Seven covers Reconstruction and the rise of Jim Crow in the South. It also looks at events happening elsewhere in the nation. To help students synthesize these two sets of events, you might have them construct parallel time lines. One time line should plot events that happened in or mainly affected the South. The other time line should plot events in the rest of the nation. Some items may appear on both time lines. Examples include passage of the 13th, 14th, and 15th Amendments. Suggest that students use the Chronology on page 184 to determine the intervals (ten-year segments? twenty-year segments?) best suited for both time lines.

Students may want to write each item on a card to be attached to one of two clotheslines that face each other. In this way, students can pivot to see what's happening in the South and in the rest of the nation.

Assessment/Sequencing   When students have completed their parallel time lines, ask them to compare progress in the South with progress in the rest of the nation. Do items on the time lines support the following claim by the author (page 152): "The South [paid for] state-supported inequality...by stagnating"? Why or why not?

USING MAPS

Book Seven talks a lot about the movements of people. People head in and out of the South. They also spill across the Great Plains. At the same time, immigrants are arriving on both the West and East coasts. To follow these events and migrations, have students locate and plot key movements on the reproducible political and relief maps provided with this guide and the study guide. Alternately, have students record this information in groups on large wall maps. Encourage students to determine which of these movements increased the diversity of our nation. Which, if any, of the movements contributed to unity? (Immigration is a good example of movement that increased diversity, while movement of people by transcontinental railroads promoted unity.)

Assessment/Analyzing Maps Assign students to review their maps. Have them study the maps and population tables on the "Population of Major Cities" maps in the Atlas of their books. Suppose they had worked for the U.S. Census Bureau in 1890. What important population patterns would they report?

WRITING HISTORY

The author hopes that students will bring history alive by retelling and adding their own stories to *A History of US*. One way to accomplish this is to ask students to set up a separate section in their history journals in which they write their own history books.

When you finish each chapter, give students time to write their own accounts of events. (Students may want to dig deeper into the past or illustrate their histories.) Point out that Joy Hakim often suggests ideas for further investigation right in the book. From time to time, call on volunteers to share their histories with the class.

Assessment/Editing Historical Writing When students have finished their own history books for Book Seven, have them exchange their books with other students. Challenge students to pick one or two chapters in their classmates' books for editing. On a separate sheet of paper, they can write suggestions for needed clarifications or other improvements. They should also note well-written or especially interesting selections. Student editors should meet with "authors" to discuss the changes. After "authors" have revised their work, call on volunteers to read their revised chapters aloud. Encourage them to note tips that helped improve their writing.

TEACHING HISTORY

As a cooperative learning activity, you can assign teams of students to teach portions of the book. Remind students that the best teaching and learning occurs when everyone is involved. Students should think beyond lectures. Encourage them to enrich instruction with pictures, poems, art, and so on. The "teachers" should also devise short homework assignments or in-class activities. At the end of the lesson, they should submit several questions to be used as part of a self-evaluation test.

Assessment/Self-Analysis If students have acted as teachers for the class, ask them to evaluate their own teaching techniques: What worked best? What they would do differently the next time?

THE BIG IDEAS

On January 3, 1867, Thaddeus Stevens, one of the leaders of the Radical Republicans, stood to address the House of Representatives. Declared Stevens:

> *Have not loyal blacks quite as good a right to choose rulers and make laws as rebel whites?…I am for Negro suffrage in every rebel State. If it be just, it should not be denied; if it be necessary, it should be adopted; if it be a punishment to traitors, they deserve it.*

Stevens felt the federal government should exert its full authority to ensure justice for former slaves. In Stevens's mind, this would never occur so long as any state could deny an individual "due process of law." He insisted that readmission of southern states to the Union hinge upon ratification of the 14th Amendment. Part 1 explores how this demand changed the course of Reconstruction—and opened the door for far-reaching changes in the civil rights of all Americans.

INTRODUCING PART 1

SETTING GOALS

Introduce Part 1 by writing "the Agony of Reconstruction" on the chalkboard. Define *agony*. Ask students to make note of those Americans who were in agony at the end of the Civil War as they read chapters 1-7.

To set goals for Part 1, tell students that they will
- learn the roles during Reconstruction of Andrew Johnson, Thaddeus Stevens, Charlotte Forten, Edmund Ross, Blanche Bruce, and Hiram Revels.
- debate whether President Johnson's impeachment was justified.
- understand how the 14th Amendment extended justice in the United States.

SETTING A CONTEXT FOR READING

Thinking About the Big Ideas   To open Part 1, read aloud the following selection from Lincoln's Second Inaugural Address.

> *With malice toward none; with charity for all,…let us strive on to…bind up the nation's wounds; to care for him who shall have borne the battle, and for his widow, and his orphan—to do all which may achieve and cherish a just, and a lasting peace.…*

Ask students to explain what Lincoln might have meant by a "just peace" for the South. Now read aloud the quote by Thaddeus Stevens on page 18. How do Stevens's ideas of justice for the South differ from those of Lincoln? Use this discussion to lead into the questions raised by the author on page 12: "How should the North treat its former enemy? Should the South be punished?" How would Lincoln answer these questions? Stevens? How would students answer them?

Comparing and Contrasting   In Chapters 1-7 author Joy Hakim compares the immediate aftermath of the Civil War in the South to that in the North and contrasts slavery with freedom, questioning what freedom means without guarantees of civil rights. To reinforce students' understanding of the economic and social effects of the end of the war on Northerners and on black and white Southerners, have them make a comparison chart as they read Chapters 1-7.

SETTING A CONTEXT IN SPACE AND TIME

Using Maps   Refer students to the map on page 26. Focus their attention on the legend. What do students think the term *white supremacy* means? *(the belief that whites are "supreme" or "higher" than other races)* Point out that this was the belief that justified slavery in the eyes of white Southerners. Challenge students to speculate on how southern states might try to re-establish this policy after the war. (Students can compare their speculations to the facts presented in Part 1.) Next, ask students to draw a two-column table in their notebooks with the headings *Events/Laws That Promoted Reconstruction* and *Events/Laws That Worked Against Reconstruction*. Direct them to fill out this chart while reading Parts 1 and 2. This will help them understand how white supremacy returned to the South.

Understanding Change Over Time   Tell the class that Reconstruction lasted until 1877. Part 1 covers the first three years. By studying the Chronology on page 184, students can see how many events were related to issues of race and equality.

1 RECONSTRUCTION MEANS REBUILDING
PAGES 12-14

NOTE TO THE TEACHER

When you see the instruction "Read...," you can interpret it in any way that fits the lesson you are creating for your students. For example, you may read aloud to the class or to small groups, you may have volunteers read aloud, or you may have the class read silently.

READING NONFICTION

Analyzing Word Choice

Ask students to reread the last paragraph on page 14 and identify the antonyms Hakim uses to describe Reconstruction. Discuss with students how these words help them determine the author's point of view toward Reconstruction. (*Her view is that Reconstruction was a difficult time with many contradictions.*)

ACTIVITIES/JOHNS HOPKINS TEAM LEARNING

See the Student Team Learning Activity on TG page 34.

NOTE FROM THE AUTHOR

Back in 1892, Woodrow Wilson served as a member of a famous committee of ten charged to look at America's schools. That committee suggested a history-centered curriculum for all children, not just the college-bound, because "it best promotes that invaluable mental power that we call judgment."

GEOGRAPHY CONNECTIONS

Have students find the eastern U.S. relief map in the back of their study guides, or distribute copies of the map from the resource pages section of this book. Have students locate and mark the southern cities mentioned in Chapter 1.

1 Class Period   **Homework: Student Study Guide p. 11**

Chapter Summary

The Civil War destroyed a way of life in the South. President Lincoln had hoped to reconstruct the region with a gentle hand. But his assassination deprived the nation of the patience and wisdom needed to heal its deep spiritual wounds.

Key Vocabulary

polyglot   Reconstruction

1. CONNECT

Start by posing the author's questions on page 12: "Did you ever lose a fight? Were you embarrassed and angry? How do these feelings help you better understand the way white Southerners felt at the end of the war?"

2. UNDERSTAND

1. Read pages 12-13. Discuss: What do the photographs tell about the South after the Civil War? (*Wounded veterans needed help and damaged buildings needed to be rebuilt.*) Suppose you were a fact finder sent South by the president in 1866. What two problems would you say were most critical? Why? (*Economic collapse, destruction of property, lack of government and order, need to help African Americans; each of these conditions threatened reunion.*)

3. CHECK UNDERSTANDING

Writing   Write a letter or journal entry from the point of view of a Southerner—a white or black civilian or a returning Confederate soldier—describing conditions in the South in 1865.

Thinking About the Chapter (Analyzing)   Refer students to the question on page 14: "Without land, without law and order, without civil rights backed by guarantees, what did *freedom* mean?" Ask students to answer the question as if they were freedmen or freedwomen in 1865. You might have students list the conditions endured by enslaved Africans. Which of these conditions were ended by the war? What new restrictions on liberty emerged?

2 WHO WAS ANDREW JOHNSON?

PAGES 15-16

3 PRESIDENTIAL RECONSTRUCTION

PAGES 17-20

1 Class Period   Homework: Student Study Guide p. 12

Chapter Summaries

Andrew Johnson had shown courage when he turned his back on sectionalism and chose loyalty to the Union instead. But his stubborn, uncompromising nature proved his undoing as President. The Freedmen's Bureau attempted to help African Americans adjust to their new lives. But in some people's eyes President Johnson was not doing enough to protect freed people.

Key Vocabulary

Seward's Folly	compromise	traitor
martial law	black codes	

1. CONNECT

Ask students to create a list of positive presidential qualities. Then create and post a want ad for a U.S. President.

2. UNDERSTAND

1. Read pages 15-16. Discuss: What strengths did Andrew Johnson bring to political office? (*good speaking ability, loyalty to Union, courage*) What weaknesses undermined his success? (*stubbornness, unwillingness to compromise*)
2. Read pages 17-20. Discuss: What was some of the work done by the Freedmen's Bureau? (*provided food, clothing, and shelter for needy people; educated freedmen and freedwomen and children*)
3. Primary Source: Distribute Resource Page 2 (TG page 105), and discuss students' answers.

3. CHECK UNDERSTANDING

Writing   Ask students to answer the question, "What was going on in the South at the start of Reconstruction?" From the perspective of a white Southerner, white Northerner, freedman or freedwoman, or President Johnson.

Thinking About the Chapter (Evaluating)   Identify and discuss the unsettled issues at the end of the war. (*Although the questions of slavery and of a state's right to leave the union had been answered officially, there were many obstacles to true freedom.*)

READING NONFICTION

Analyzing Graphic Aids

Have students analyze the words and images in the political cartoons featuring Andrew Johnson on pages 15-16 to determine which one is more sympathetic to Johnson and why. Ask: Is a parrot a positive characterization for a person? (*no*) What words does a parrot usually say? (*A parrot repeats a limited vocabulary.*) What are the words on the Union suit on page 16? (*names of states*) What is Johnson trying to do? (*mend the Union suit; mend the Union*)

LINKING DISCIPLINES

Geography/Math

Have students locate Alaska on the U.S. map in the Atlas. Then, using information in the feature on page 16, ask students to calculate how many acres of land Seward purchased in 1867. (*Multiply the total cost of $7,200,000 by 100 to get the cost in cents—720,000,000 cents—and then divide that total by two cents per acre to get the answer of about 360,000,000 acres.*)

READING NONFICTION

Analyzing Text Features

Have partners read the vocabulary notes for *radical, nullify,* and *veto* on page 22. Then ask them to locate these words in the text. Have partners begin a vocabulary list for this book by listing each vocabulary word explained in a side note, writing a definition, and writing a sentence that uses the word in context.

MEETING INDIVIDUAL NEEDS

Visual learners will benefit from a chart of constitutional amendments. This will help them to see a continuum extending from rights guaranteed in the Bill of Rights (Amendments 1-10) to those spelled out in Amendments 13 and 14.

CHAPTER 4 · SLAVERY AND STATES' RIGHTS
PAGES 21-23

1 Class Period   **Homework: Student Study Guide p. 13**

Chapter Summary

Two amendments to the Constitution addressed the issues over which the Civil War was fought. The 13th Amendment abolished slavery, and the 14th Amendment limited states' rights and made the federal government the guardian of individual liberties.

Key Vocabulary

nullify   unalienable (inalienable)
states' rights   civil rights

1. CONNECT

Define *civil rights* as rights guaranteed by the Constitution and Congress. List some of these rights on the chalkboard. Discuss with students how the civil rights of freedmen and freedwomen were denied during Reconstruction.

2. UNDERSTAND

1. Read aloud the 13th Amendment on page 21. Have students rephrase the text in their own words. (*Slavery is illegal. Congress can pass laws to enforce the amendment.*)
2. Read pages 21-23. Discuss answers to the author's questions: "If you are free and can't vote, are you really free? If some laws still restrict your movement, are you free?" (*For African Americans who had been enslaved,* freedom *meant equality before the law.*)
3. Ask: How did the 14th Amendment affect the balance of power between state and federal governments? (*took power from the states by forbidding them to deprive citizens of life, liberty, or property without due process of law; gave the Supreme Court the power to limit states' rights.*)

3. CHECK UNDERSTANDING

Writing   Have small groups of students brainstorm examples supporting the author's statement that "freedom means choices and responsibilities." Then students should write a paragraph describing what freedom means to them.

Thinking About the Chapter (Evaluating)   Have students define the importance of the 14th Amendment. Ask: How did the 14th Amendment help protect the inalienable rights of all citizens? Have students provide details from the chapter to support their views.

CHAPTER 5 · CONGRESSIONAL RECONSTRUCTION

PAGES 24–27

1 Class Period   Homework: Student Study Guide p. 14

Chapter Summary

In 1867, Radical Republicans in Congress took control of Reconstruction. Federal troops marched South and opened the doors of government to newly enfranchised blacks.

Key Vocabulary

illiterate   integrity

1. CONNECT

Compare the titles of Chapters 5 and 3. Explain that some members of Congress considered "presidential reconstruction" to be a failure. Then read aloud the first paragraph of Chapter 5.

2. UNDERSTAND

1. Read Chapter 5. Discuss: Who were some of the Northerners who headed South? Why did each group go? (*soldiers: to guarantee the freedom of black Southerners; carpetbaggers: to help govern or to turn a quick profit; Freedmen's Bureau workers: to help African Americans freed from slavery*) How did the Reconstruction Act change politics in the South and the North? (*South: black men were elected to local, state, and national offices. North: too few black voters; could not overcome prejudice.*)
2. Map: Refer students to Resource Page 1 (TG page 104) to see how the South was divided into five military districts. Point out that each district was occupied by armed troops. Ask: What was the effect of military occupation on white Southerners? (*Possible answers: made them angry at not being able to vote while black citizens could; difficult to accept what was happening; clung to racist myths*)

3. CHECK UNDERSTANDING

Writing   Have students write a letter home from the point of view of a Northern soldier, carpetbagger, or Freedmen's Bureau employee describing why they have come to the South in 1867.

Thinking About the Chapter (Synthesizing)   Discuss the difference between presidential reconstruction and congressional reconstruction. Have students identify how each affected the South. (*President Johnson trusted the states to undertake reconstruction; Congress sent troops and passed laws to impose reconstruction on the states.*)

READING NONFICTION

Analyzing Text Organization

Have students reread the first four paragraphs in Chapter 5 (pages 24-25). Elicit that the author is describing Northerners who went South during Congressional Reconstruction. Ask: How does the author's organization of the paragraphs' information provide a balanced picture of these Northerners? (*Paragraph 1 gives reasons why Northerners went South; paragraphs 2 and 3 give details that support Southerners' negative attitudes; paragraph 4 restates with concrete examples her contention that most Northerners went South to help.*)

READING NONFICTION

Analyzing Point of View

Have students locate words and phrases used to describe Thaddeus Stevens in Chapter 6. (*poor, handicapped, fiercely honest, handsome, intelligent, didn't care what others thought, abolitionist*) Ask: what conclusions can you draw about the author's view of Stevens?

MEETING INDIVIDUAL NEEDS

Assign a group of students to do further research on W. E. B. DuBois and Booker T. Washington and the lasting impact of these two influential African Americans. The following web site contains links to writings by the two men and assessments of their lives and influence:

www.pbs.org/wgbh/pages/frontline/shows/ race/etc/road.html

CHAPTER 6

THADDEUS STEVENS: RADICAL

PAGES 28-31

1 Class Period   **Homework: Student Study Guide p. 15**

Chapter Summary

Thaddeus Stevens's unrelenting and uncompromising resolve to win justice for African Americans led to the impeachment of President Andrew Johnson—one of the great trials in U.S. history.

Key Vocabulary

impeach   high crimes   misdemeanors

1. CONNECT

Ask students to define *honesty*. Does it mean always telling the truth, even when it is unpopular to do so? Ask: How likely is it to find truly honest people in politics? Do people really admire honesty in politicians?

2. UNDERSTAND

1. Read pages 28-29. Discuss: What character traits helped Thaddeus Stevens become a strong politician? (*a good mind, fierce honesty, a good business sense, a commitment to the principle of equality for all*)
2. Read pages 30-31. Discuss: What major difference separated Stevens and Johnson? (*Stevens felt the federal government should ensure fair treatment of black people. Johnson felt that job belonged to the states.*)
3. Read the feature on page 30. Discuss the process and ask students to outline the roles of the House and the Senate. Use this open-ended discussion to bridge Chapters 6 and 7.

3. CHECK UNDERSTANDING

Writing   People either loved or hated Thaddeus Stevens. Have students choose a position and write a short obituary for him.

Thinking About the Chapter (Analyzing)   Lead students to recognize that the passions that brought on the Civil War still existed after the war's end. Have them trace the mix of practical issues and fanaticism that led to the impeachment of President Johnson.

7 IMPEACHING A PRESIDENT

PAGES 32–35

1 Class Period   Homework: Student Study Guide p. 15

Chapter Summary

The fate of President Johnson rested upon a single vote. In an act of courage, Senator Edmund Ross of Kansas voted against impeachment and in favor of preserving the balance of power between Congress and the presidency.

Key Vocabulary

conviction   bigotry   balance of power

1. CONNECT

Explain to students that Chapter 6 ends with what is called a "cliffhanger," because the final question leaves the reader dangling. Ask students to formulate the question in their own words. (*Possible responses: Was President Johnson impeached? Was he convicted and thrown out of office?*)

2. UNDERSTAND

1. Read through the second paragraph on page 33. Invite a pair of students to present a dramatic reading starting from "Picture the scene" through the fifth paragraph on page 34. Discuss: Why was there so much pressure on Edmund Ross? (*He was the only senator who had not stated in advance how he would vote, and the necessary two-thirds vote for impeachment was one vote short.*)
2. Ask students to suppose that Ross had voted for impeachment. How would his vote have affected the system of checks and balances? Why? (*It would have made Congress the most powerful branch of government, because it would have set a precedent of Congress removing elected leaders on the basis of personality rather than illegal conduct.*)

3. CHECK UNDERSTANDING

Writing   Ask students to imagine they are Edmund Ross and write a letter to a constituent about the impeachment trial. The letter should explain why Ross voted according to his conscience instead of according to the will of many Kansas voters.

Thinking About the Chapter (Evaluating)   Elicit from students a definition of "high crimes and misdemeanors." Then have them give examples of the crimes for which a president can be impeached. Make sure students understand the difference between breaking the law and acting in an unpopular way. Ask: Was President Johnson's impeachment justified?

LINKING DISCIPLINES

History/Math

Invite a team of students to determine how many senators there were in 1868 and to calculate how many constituted the two-thirds majority necessary to find the President guilty.

MEETING INDIVIDUAL NEEDS

Invite a team of students with strong research skills to investigate and report on the impeachment of President Clinton in 1999.

READING NONFICTION

Organizing and Interpreting Information from Outlines

Before students read Chapter 6, give them practice in organizing and interpreting information from an outline. Copy the outline below onto the chalkboard and ask students what they can learn from reading the outline alone. Help them see that the outline tells the story as well as organizes the information. (*Students can see that charges were brought against Johnson, that Stevens played a major role, that there was a trial, and that the vote was against impeachment.*) After students read the chapter, have them work in groups to add a third level of information to the outline.

Impeaching a President

I. The Charges

    A. Constitutional Process

    B. Opinions of Thaddeus Stevens

    C. Public Outcry

II. The Trial

    A. Debate in the House of

       Representatives

    B. Vote Against Impeachment

III. The Effects

    A. Reactions against Thaddeus Stevens

    B. Constitutional Concerns

JOHNS HOPKINS TEAM LEARNING

ARE WE EQUAL?

1 CLASS PERIOD

FOCUS ACTIVITY

Write "What Equality Means to Me" on the chalkboard and ask students to compose an essay, poem, or story with that title.

STUDENT TEAM LEARNING ACTIVITY/READING AND PARAPHRASING DOCUMENTS

1. Divide the class into teams, then pose these questions: Are we equal? Who is included in "we"?

2. Write the following questions on the chalkboard and have students answer them using **Think-Team-Share** after reading pages 9 and 10 of Book Seven:
- With what radical new idea did America begin? (*that all people are created equal*)
- What do we as Americans mean when we say that "we are created equal"? (*All people have certain rights that we hold equally. No one has more rights than anyone else, and no one can take our rights from us.*)
- In what important document are these rights listed? (*Declaration of Independence*)
- What are those rights? *(life, liberty, the pursuit of happiness)*
- Why is America still an experiment? (*Americans are still striving and struggling to ensure equal rights to all, including minorities, immigrants, and women; to define the right to life in issues such as capital punishment and new medical technology; to ensure liberty and freedom to all people; and to protect the right of all to pursue happiness.*)

3. Circulate and Monitor Visit each team to help students read the text and discuss the questions.

4. Use **Numbered Heads** for the teams to share their answers with the class. If necessary, clarify the concepts concerning America as an experiment in democracy and its goals to secure justice and equality for all people.

5. Read to your students the passage from the Declaration of Independence on pages 10 and 11. Ask each team to create sentence strips paraphrasing the quotation. If necessary, provide dictionaries or definitions of the difficult words in the quotation.

6. Sharing Information Using **Numbered Heads** have each team read the paraphrases to the class and discuss how well each paraphrase captures the meaning of the Declaration of Independence. Display the sentence strips in the classroom.

ASSESSMENT

Part 1 Check-Up   Use Check-Up 1 (TG page 97) to assess student learning in Part 1.

ALTERNATE ASSESSMENT
Use this activity to help students link the big ideas across chapters.

Making Connections   Assign groups of students to draw a chart comparing Presidential Reconstruction with Congressional Reconstruction. To get them started, draw a four-column chart on the chalkboard with the headings *Type of Reconstruction, Goals, Methods,* and *Results.* In column 1, list *Presidential* and *Congressional,* and ask students to complete the chart.

DEBATING THE ISSUES
The topics below can stimulate debate.

1. Resolved   That slaves should be paid for all their years of past suffering and work. You might conduct this debate in the form of a courtroom scene in which some students take the part of African Americans who testify about the amount and/or value of their labor while they were enslaved. Lawyers might also include some of the "legal eagles" mentioned on page 17.

2. Resolved   The author notes on page 33 that, aside from the Bill of Rights, the 14th Amendment is the most important of all the Constitutional Amendments. Assign students to study other amendments prior to organizing the debate. Students debating the *con* side should select at least two other amendments they believe are more important than the 14th.

MAKING ETHICAL JUDGMENTS
The following question asks students to consider an issue of ethics.

The impeachment trial of Andrew Johnson was decided by the vote of Senator Ross, who voted against the wishes of many of his constituents and, in his words, "for the highest good of the country." Have students discuss whether Senator Ross acted ethically by voting as he did.

PROJECTS AND ACTIVITIES
Writing Historical Fiction   Working individually or in small groups, students can write fictional accounts of a former Confederate soldier's homecoming. Stories can be written from the point of view of the soldier, his family, and those he had formerly enslaved. Writers should include a description of the physical destruction to the South and dialogues that reveal characters' feelings about the war. Allow time for students to read their stories aloud. (Some students might wish to write and enact dramatic scenes, instead.)

USING THE RUBRICS

To assess these writing assignments, group projects, and activities, scoring rubrics have been provided at the back of this to this Teaching Guide. Be sure to explain the rubrics to your students.

Analyzing a Quote

Tell students that black historian and scholar W. E. B. DuBois summed up Reconstruction in the following words:

> The slave went free; stood a brief moment in the sun; then moved back again toward slavery.

Call on students to state in their own words Dubois's opinion of Reconstruction. In the years between 1865 and 1876, how did African Americans "stand in the sun"? What events pushed them back toward slavery? Tell students that in Part 2 they will learn how Reconstruction came to an end.

Analyzing a Quote   In 1866, Frederick Douglass declared:

> The arm of the Federal government is long, but it is far too short to protect the rights of individuals in the interior of distant States. They must have the power to protect themselves, or they will go unprotected, in spite of all the laws the Federal government can put upon the national statute-book.

Read this quote aloud. Then ask students to name examples of injustice that Douglass might have used to support his opinion. What power might Douglass have thought was necessary to protect blacks? *(the power to elect local officials to protect them)*

Drawing a Flowchart   You can assign more advanced students to study the impeachment process by studying Article I, Sections 2 and 3 in the Constitution. Ask them to make flowcharts to illustrate the impeachment process, and then to use the charts to explain the process to the class. Next, call on volunteers to use these flowcharts to trace impeachment proceedings against Andrew Johnson. At what stage in the process were proceedings halted? Suppose Johnson had been impeached? What would have happened next?

THE BIG IDEAS

In 1875, near the end of Reconstruction, Ralph Waldo Emerson wrote:

We hoped that in the peace…a great expansion would follow in the mind of the country, grand views in every direction.…But the energy of the nation seems to have expended itself.

The passions of civil war and the fury of Radical Reconstruction had left the nation exhausted. The 13th, 14th, and 15th Amendments were enduring accomplishments. But federal enforcement lay nearly a century in the future. Part 2 describes the twilight of Reconstruction and the retreat of Northern troops from the South.

PART 2 — RETREAT FROM THE SOUTH

INTRODUCING PART 2

SETTING GOALS

Review the features of the 13th, 14th, and 15th Amendments. Discuss how the provisions of these amendments were enforced. (*by federal troops*) Ask students to speculate what opposition there might be to these Amendments and who would be interested in undermining them. (*former slave owners, white Southern politicians, Northerners who saw these Amendments as a threat to the racial status quo*)

To set goals for Part 2, tell students that they will
• discover what the right to vote meant to freedmen in the South.
• describe some of the economic gains made by freedmen and freedwomen under Reconstruction.
• determine the forces that ultimately wiped out the political and economic gains of black Southerners under Reconstruction.

SETTING A CONTEXT FOR READING

Thinking About the Big Ideas   Write the title of Part 2 on the chalkboard: "Retreat from the South." Ask students what *retreat* means to them. (*going backward or withdrawing*) Who would most likely be retreating from this region? (*federal troops, carpetbaggers, Radical Republicans*) If these groups did withdraw from the South, what might happen to the struggle for equal justice for blacks? Why? What changes would this bring about for blacks and whites in the South?

Evaluating the Author's Purpose   Read aloud the titles of Chapters 8 and 9. Discuss with students what the titles suggest about the chapters' contents. (*The focus will be on a specific place and on a specific person.*) Now read the title of Chapter 10, "A Failed Revolution." Students should understand that this suggests the writer's purpose is to give a wider view of events than in Chapters 8 and 9. Ask students to compare the advantages of a narrow focus and a wider focus in presenting history.

SETTING A CONTEXT IN SPACE AND TIME

Linking Geography to Politics   Refer students back to the map on page 26. Tell them to substitute the words *Democratic power* for *white supremacy* in the legend. With this change in mind, what can they infer about the shift in political power in the South by 1877? *(It had shifted to the Democrats.)* Next, challenge students to speculate on reasons white Southerners might support the Democratic party. (*Lead students to recognize the link between the Republicans and Reconstruction.*) Tell students that Part 2 traces the retreat of the Republicans from the South.

Understanding Change Over Time   Reconstruction forms a distinct era in United States history. Ask students to recall its span. (*1865-1877*) Have students skim the Chronology on page 184 to find events relating to issues of race and equality after 1877. Which ones prove that Radical Reconstruction was, as the author suggests, "a failed revolution"? *(the 1883 Plessy v. Ferguson decision and the 1892 exposé of lynching)*

CHAPTER 8

WELCOME TO MEETING STREET

PAGES 36-39

1 Class Period   **Homework: Student Study Guide p. 16**

Chapter Summary

Reconstruction legislatures prompted some people to talk of "America's Second Revolution." Slowly but surely, former Confederate officers and officials organized "Redeemer" governments that pushed blacks out of politics.

Key Vocabulary

ubiquitous   redeemer governments

1. CONNECT

Remind students that the Reconstruction Act gave freedmen (not women) the right to vote. Ask students to consider what that right meant to people who under slavery had had no rights at all. (*The vote meant that freedmen had political power—they could elect representatives or run for office.*)

2. UNDERSTAND

1. Read up to the second paragraph on page 38. Discuss: What was remarkable about the 1868 South Carolina constitutional convention? (*the number of talented black representatives*) What was the purpose of the convention? (*to write a new South Carolina state constitution so South Carolina could be readmitted to the Union*)
2. Map: Have students refer to their copies of Resource Page 1 (TG page 104) and note the date South Carolina and the other states were readmitted to the Union.
3. Read the rest of the chapter. Discuss: What did the Reconstruction legislatures achieve? (*voted for free public schools, built roads, treated former Confederates fairly*) How did the "Redeemer" governments seize power? (*by using fear and intimidation to keep blacks from the polls*)

3. CHECK UNDERSTANDING

Writing   Ask students to write an editorial for or against the idea of taking land from Confederates and giving it to freedmen. Have students refer to the feature on page 37.

Thinking About the Chapter (Evaluating)   Discuss the connection between the large black populations in the South and the interracial Reconstruction governments. (*With their right to vote protected, black Southerners had the power to elect black officials.*)

LINKING DISCIPLINES

Art/Language Arts

Have students look at the picture on page 39. Explain that the title of the picture is "The Shackle Broken by the Genius of Freedom." Have students create other titles for the painting based on information about Robert Elliott (page 36) and their understanding of his words in Congress (page 37) on the occasion the painting celebrates.

ACTIVITY/JOHNS HOPKINS TEAM LEARNING

See Student Team Learning Activity on TG page 42.

Analyzing Primary and Secondary Sources

Have partners identify the primary sources in the chapter. (*all the visual information and the diary entries*) Ask students how the photo on page 41 and the photo on page 42 of the community in front of Hurricane Garden Cottage help verify and illustrate the secondary source material in the chapter. (*The photos illustrate the author's information about the black community from their beginning as slave workers on the plantation to being free workers and participants in the plantation.*)

NOTE FROM THE AUTHOR

I've written a storyteller's history. It is intellectual history. It starts with the belief that children can handle complex ideas and that they enjoy being challenged. It is a history that celebrates our free, democratic form of government. Some critics may find it jingoistic. I don't think it is. I don't neglect the horrors and mistakes of our past. But there is a big difference in forms of government, and I believe we are fortunate in our heritage. I tell my readers that. I also tell them that this is my opinion and they are free to challenge it. I'm told that the books provoke much discussion. That is my intention.

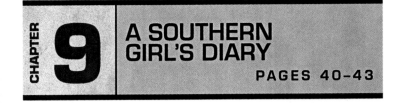

CHAPTER 9 · A SOUTHERN GIRL'S DIARY
PAGES 40–43

1 Class Period   **Homework: Student Study Guide p. 17**

Chapter Summary

African Americans who had been enslaved, such as the Montgomery family, briefly tasted the joy of land ownership and free enterprise. Their success made the reconfiscation of lands by former Confederates even more bitter—and more unjust.

Key Vocabulary
patent   subverted

1. CONNECT

Open your discussion of Chapter 9 by asking: What did Congressional Reconstruction give to freedmen that they did not have under slavery? (*political power*) Ask what freedmen and freedwomen needed besides political power to be truly free. (*economic power*)

2. UNDERSTAND

1. Read the chapter. Discuss: How did the Montgomery family gain control of Davis Bend? (*They first rented the land, then raised the money to buy it.*) What freedoms did African Americans enjoy at Davis Bend? (*the right to own property and to share in the profits of their labor; the right to elect judges, sheriffs, and political leaders*)
2. How did the Montgomery family lose Davis Bend? (*Power shifts allowed Jefferson Davis to reconfiscate the land.*)

3. CHECK UNDERSTANDING

Writing   Ask students to write an advertisement to attract freedmen and women to settle at Davis Bend.

Thinking About the Chapter (Analyzing)   Have students work in groups to use information in Chapter 9 to create a profile of one of the following people: Mary Virginia Montgomery, Benjamin Montgomery, Jefferson Davis, Joseph Davis.

CHAPTER 10

A FAILED REVOLUTION

PAGES 44-48

1 Class Period   Homework: Student Study Guide p. 18

Chapter Summary

In 1877, a political deal led President Rutherford Hayes to call an end to Reconstruction. By the end of the decade, black Southerners found themselves under the lash of a new master—a fool named Jim Crow.

Key Vocabulary

sharecropping   poll tax   lynching
segregation   Jim Crow

1. CONNECT

Remind students that in Chapter 8, the author refers to the "Second American Revolution." Chapter 10 is called "A Failed Revolution." Discuss the meaning of *revolution* and make sure students understand how profoundly revolutionary an equitable Southern society would have been.

2. UNDERSTAND

1. Read pages 44–46. Discuss: What problems did Reconstruction cause in the minds of many white Southerners? (*forced landowners to pay for improvements voted in by black lawmakers; raised the idea that perhaps Confederate soldiers died for a mistaken notion about slavery*) How did white Southerners move to restrict the rights of blacks? (*poll taxes, lynching, segregation*)
2. Read pages 47–48. Discuss: How did Republicans and Redeemer Democrats differ in their view of the role of government? (*Democrats did not approve of an active government that tried to improve conditions for all people.*)
3. Primary Source: Copy and distribute Resource Page 3 (TG page 106). Connect the information about what was happening in Alabama with information in the feature on page 48.

3. CHECK UNDERSTANDING

Writing   Ask students to write letters as Northerners, explaining why they are leaving the South in 1877.

Thinking About the Chapter (Synthesizing)   Discuss answers to the author's questions about Eric Foner's quotation in the margin on page 45: "Was the idea [of a struggle for equal rights] reborn? When?" Ask students to share what they know about the history of the civil rights struggle; discuss the connections between the struggle of the 1950s and 1960s and Reconstruction.

READING NONFICTION

Analyzing Rhetorical Devices

Point out the parenthetical remark made by the author near the end of page 47. ("This is where studying history helps you....") Ask students if they think the "you" in that sentence means them—the readers. How about when she says, "But don't be too hard on the South"? Discuss with students that the author occasionally addresses the reader directly. Ask students how it affects their reading. Does it make them stop and think?

MEETING INDIVIDUAL NEEDS

Some students may have difficulty understanding the connection between government corruption and economic chaos (page 45). Work as a class to connect this "economic chaos" with "white supremacy" (page 47) as explanations for the South's becoming, as the author says on page 47, "the poorest section of the nation."

JOHNS HOPKINS TEAM LEARNING

TWO TYPES OF POWER

JOHNS HOPKINS
U N I V E R S I T Y

1 CLASS PERIOD

FOCUS ACTIVITY

Ask students to consider this situation: You are a freed black person in the South during Reconstruction. Consider the situation in the South and your rights as assured by the three Reconstruction amendments to the Constitution. Use **Think-Pair-Share** to elicit answers to the question: What are your two most important goals?

Help students conclude that the two greatest needs of freedmen and freedwomen during Reconstruction were economic power and political power.

- Economic Power: Former slaves needed to become financially independent and self-sufficient in order to feed, clothe, and house themselves. Blacks could not depend on former owners now that they were free, and the Freedmen's Bureau gave limited help. Because the key to economic independence in the South was to own farmland, blacks struggled to achieve such ownership, but instead were forced to become sharecroppers.
- Political Power: Freedmen needed the right to vote to elect local and state officials sympathetic to their cause. Through equal representation, black Southerners could pass laws and elect local officials to protect them from discrimination and violence.

STUDENT TEAM LEARNING ACTIVITY/INTERVIEWING TO GAIN INFORMATION

1. Divide the class into teams. Within teams have students form two partnerships—one to read Chapter 8 and the other to read Chapter 9. Each partnership will then tell the story of its chapter through a mock television news interview. One partner role playing a television reporter interviews the other partner who role plays a major figure in the chapter. Be sure that students understand that an interview makes use of a question-and-answer format. Partners plan their interview questions and answers using information in their chapter.

2. Circulate and Monitor   As team partners plan and present their television interview to their teammates, help them develop good interview questions and accurate, complete answers to convey the story of their chapter. Use a timer to limit presentations to three minutes.

3. Sharing Information   Each partnership will present their interview to the other students on their team. Following the presentations, have teams briefly discuss these questions:
- How does each chapter illustrate a way in which black Southerners attempted to secure equality and freedom? (*Chapter 8: political power—voting and electing representatives—to promote equality and freedom. Chapter 9: economic power—the financial success of a black farming community that actually purchased and owned land.*)
- Why were both political and economic power necessary for black Southerners? (*Civil rights needed to be protected through state and federal government, and freed slaves needed to be paid a fair wage or own farmland in order to be economically free.*)

ASSESSMENT

Part 2 Check-Up Use Check-Up 2 (TG page 98) to assess student learning in Part 2.

ALTERNATE ASSESSMENT
Ask students to write an essay answering one of the following questions, which link the big ideas across chapters:

1. Making Connections What was the connection between political corruption and the end of Reconstruction? (*Corruption became so widespread that it distracted Northerners from the struggle for civil rights in the South.*)

2. Making Connections What was the connection between white supremacy and slow economic recovery in the South? (*Slow recovery stifled creativity, limited the workforce, and discouraged immigrants and big industries from heading into the region.*)

DEBATING THE ISSUES
The topic below can be used to stimulate debate.

Resolved That the Confederacy lost the Civil War but won the battle against Reconstruction. (Appoint some students to defend the legal precedents set in place during Reconstruction, particularly the 13th, 14th, and 15th Amendments. Have others point out ways in which white supremacists undermined the principles of justice for all and "due process of law.")

MAKING ETHICAL JUDGMENTS
The following activity asks students to consider issues of ethics.

Thaddeus Stevens volunteered to defend Jefferson Davis. Why do you think Stevens took this position? Do you agree? (*Stevens believed in universal justice. He was not afraid to take an unpopular stand if he thought it was right and just.*) You might ask some of your students to review John Adams's defense of soldiers involved in the Boston Massacre and present their answers to the question: How were the ethical decisions faced by Adams and Stevens similar?

PROJECTS AND ACTIVITIES
Writing a News Story Working individually or in groups, students can imagine they are reporters for a northern newspaper. Their task is to cover the South Carolina constitutional convention. Tell students to be sure to answer the six questions: *Who? What? When? Where? Why? How?* To get students started, you might distribute copies of the article headline and lead sentence.
> *Integration Comes to South Carolina by (student's name)*
> *Charleston, SC, January 14, 1868. The black delegates who walked into the fashionable Charleston Clubhouse rewrote history today.*

USING THE RUBRICS

To assess these writing assignments, group projects, and activities, scoring rubrics have been provided at the back of this Teaching Guide. Be sure to explain the rubrics to your students.

Stating the Problem

Read aloud a description of the mood among freed people written by a black Texan in 1879:

> There are no words which can fully express...the real condition of my people throughout the south, nor how deeply and keenly they feel the necessity of fleeing from the...long pent-up hatred of their old masters which they feel assured will...burst loose like the pent-up fires of a volcano and crush them if they remain here many years longer.

What problem did the writer foresee for black Southerners at the end of Reconstruction? (*pent-up anger of former slave owners*) What action does the speaker feel they must take? (*flee the region*) Tell students that in the late 1870s many blacks saw a new escape route—flight onto the unsettled Great Plains. Expansion into the West, a region claimed by Native Americans, forms the subject of Part 3.

Using Historical Imagination   Jefferson Davis never stood trial. But ask students to suppose he had. Have them design a skit in which they speculate on how the trial might have progressed. Tell students to select one of the African American "legal eagles" mentioned in Chapter 3 as prosecutor. Suggest that Thaddeus Stevens serve as the defense attorney. Other students can take the parts of the interracial jury pictured on page 40. Still other students can act as witnesses. At the end of the skit, allow time for members of the jury to present their verdict.

Designing a Historical Marker   Direct students to prepare historical markers for the sites of the black communities at Davis Bend and Mound Bayou.

Drawing Political Cartoons   Refer students to the political cartoons in Chapter 10. Then have them work in small groups to design political cartoons expressing their opinions of Reconstruction.

Research Project-Role Play   Divide the class into small groups. Have each group pretend to be a family of newly freed slaves in the South during Reconstruction. Tell them they will need to choose the best plan for their family's future from the following: Remain in the South, move to a Northern industrial city, or move to the Western frontier. Have groups brainstorm pros and cons for each choice, and decide what to do. Have the groups research the likely opportunities for freed black men, women and children in their region of choice during reconstruction, including education, work, equal rights, and community. Have them jump forward five years in time and present to the class a family history since leaving the plantation.

Library/Media Center Research   Have the students investigate and research the lives of Buffalo Soldiers. Using library/media center, have students write a story about a day in the life of a Buffalo Soldier, utilizing photographs and personal histories as research.

THE BIG IDEAS

Native Americans saw the sprawling Great Plains differently than did the settlers who moved west and who took the land from them. Explained Chief Luther Standing Bear of the Oglala Sioux:

> *We did not think of the great open plains...as "wild." Only to the white man was nature a "wilderness."...To us it was tame....Not until [settlers] from the east came and with brutal frenzy heaped injustices upon us...was it "wild" for us.*

In the late 1800s, the trail of broken treaties that had robbed Native American peoples of their lands reached the Great Plains. Part 3 describes the changes that settlement of the Great Plains brought to Native Americans—and to the nation as a whole.

PART 3 | BATTLE FOR THE WEST

INTRODUCING PART 3

SETTING GOALS

Introduce Part 3 by having students read the titles of the eight chapters in Part 3. Then have students predict changes that came to the West in the years following the Civil War. Refer students first to the poster on page 49 and then to the map on page 55. What changes can they infer from these sources? (*the settlement of prairies where Native Americans lived*)

To set goals for Part 3, tell students that they will
- chart a variety of points of view about the West.
- discover what pressures affected Native Americans' ways of life in the West after the Civil War.
- debate the inevitability of Native Americans having to give up their traditional lands and lifeways.

SETTING A CONTEXT FOR READING

Thinking About the Big Ideas Ask students to put themselves in the place of Native Americans at the time. How would they feel at the sight of cattle trails, railroads, and homesteaders crossing their land? (*anger, a sense of loss*) How would settlers feel about the same sights? (*pride, a sense of accomplishment and excitement*) You may want to read aloud the quote from Chief Luther Standing Bear above. How did Native Americans and settlers view the plains? How might these different views lead to "injustices" for Native Americans?

Identifying Points of View In Chapters 11-18, author Joy Hakim introduces a variety of people with different points of view about the West. As students read through the chapters, have them create a chart listing various people and their points of view about the West. Students should use the sidebars as well as the chapter text in creating their charts.

SETTING A CONTEXT IN SPACE AND TIME

Using Maps   To set the stage for the environmental changes that settlement brought to the Great Plains and the West, have students prepare the western U.S. relief map found in the back of their study guides or distribute copies of the map from the resource pages section of this guide. Have students title the map "Battle for the West" and trace state outlines and label the major landforms shown on the map, using the map on page 75 as a guide. Students will use this map for "Geography Connections" activities throughout Part 3. Ask what landforms bounded the Great Plains on the east and west. (*Mississippi River and Rocky Mountains*) What nations set its northern and southern limits? (*Canada and Mexico*) Next, ask students to identify some of the forms of wildlife shown on the map on page 75. Then request a volunteer to look up *prairie* in a dictionary. (*meadow or area of rolling grasslands*) Why would this environment support such a wide variety of wildlife? (*provided a huge grazing area*) Challenge students to speculate on what changes settlers would bring to this environment. Save the speculations for review as students work their way through Part 3.

Understanding Change Over Time   To provide an overview of the effect of settlement on Native Americans, have students turn to the time line on page 88. What has happened to Native Americans since the arrival of the first European settlers? (*Their independence has steadily diminished.*) What items in the time line show the restriction of Native American rights during the 1800s? When did Native Americans finally become U.S. citizens? Remind students of another name used to describe Native Americans—*First Americans.* What irony does this time line point out? (*Although Native Americans were the first to settle what is now the United States, they were the last to receive citizenship.*)

11 MEANWHILE, OUT WEST

PAGES 49-51

1 Class Period   **Homework: Student Study Guide p. 19**

Chapter Summary
No sooner had the Civil War ended than settlers spilled onto the Great Plains. Here settlers battled Native Americans and the environment to turn the prairies into the nation's "breadbasket."

Key Vocabulary
capital   depression

1. CONNECT

Have a discussion with students about the term "out West." Using the map of the United States in the Atlas, determine who would use the term to refer to the West. (*people in the East*) Ask: Why wouldn't Native Americans refer to the Great Plains as "out West"? (*because they had inhabited the West for a long time*)

2. UNDERSTAND

1. Read pages 49-51. Discuss: What was the war in the West about? (*control of the land*) What led settlers to move onto Native American lands? (*Many held mistaken ideas about Native Americans and who had rights to the land. An economic depression and lack of land in the East also pushed people onto the Plains.*)
2. Map: Refer to the map on page 55 to answer the author's question: How could Chicago grow into an important port? (*Ask students to locate Chicago on the Great Lakes. Note all the rail links to major rivers.*)
3. Read the Whitman poem on page 51. Discuss: What types of growth does Whitman mention in his poem? (*growth of cities, growth of commerce, growth of communication, growth of transportation, etc.*) What about the Native Americans? (*There doesn't seem to be a place for them.*)

3. CHECK UNDERSTANDING

Writing   Look at the photograph of Lincoln, Nebraska in 1872, on page 51. Write a letter from Lincoln describing it to a friend "back East," encouraging the Easterner to move west.

Thinking About the Chapter (Hypothesizing)   Encourage students to connect the author's statement on page 51 that "before long the nation would be an industrial and agricultural giant" with Walt Whitman's lines on the same page.

READING NONFICTION
Analyzing Point of View
Ask partners to write a sentence describing the author's point of view toward the displacement of Native Americans from their land. Then ask students why her point of view is easy to figure out. (*She states clearly that Indians had been fighting wars for their land for years and that all the treaties had been broken.*) Ask: Why does Joy Hakim state her opinion at this point in the book? (*She is beginning to discuss events in the West, which is where the majority of Indians then were.*)

GEOGRAPHY CONNECTIONS
Have students continue the "Battle for the West" activity described on TG page 46. Have students identify and label the Great Plains states of their maps.

HISTORY ARCHIVES
A History of US Sourcebook
#60, From John Wesley Powell, *Report on the Arid Region of the West* (1878)

GEOGRAPHY CONNECTIONS

Have students continue the "Battle for the West" activity described on TG page 46. Referring to the map on page 55 of their books, have students locate and mark on their maps the Chisholm Trail and Goodnight-Loving Trail, including cities, rivers, and landforms along the route. Have students create a chart comparing information about the physical features of both trails that would have been useful in planning a cattle drive.

READING NONFICTION

Analyzing Graphic Aids

Refer to the map on page 55 and ask students what the colored lines running south to north show. (*cattle trails*) The spoked black lines running east and west? (*railroads*) Discuss how these two features are related (*The map shows which trails cattle from Texas might follow to intersect with railroad lines leading to Chicago.*)

CHAPTER 12 — RIDING THE TRAIL

PAGES 52-57

1 Class Period   Homework: Student Study Guide p. 19

Chapter Summary

For a brief period, much of the Great Plains belonged to the Texas longhorns and cattle herders who rode the open range. The meeting of cattle trails and railroad lines created "cow towns" still famous in western lore—Abilene, Dodge City, Wichita, and others.

Key Vocabulary
range   longhorns

1. CONNECT

Ask students to list the words they associate with cowboys. Explain that as they read through the chapter, they will meet some of these words and add others that describe the cowboys' experience in the 1870s and 1880s.

2. UNDERSTAND

1. Read up to the second paragraph of page 53. Discuss: What developments helped turn cattle raising into a profitable business? (*westward expansion of railroads; opening of cattle trails to shipping centers such as Abilene; development of refrigerated rail cars; demand for beef*)
2. Read pages 53-57. Discuss: What hardships did cowboys face along the trail? (*bad weather, attacks by Native Americans and rustlers, thirst, stampedes, etc.*) Why was there greater democracy on the cattle trails than in other areas of American life? (*because people were judged by their ability to do the job, not the color of their skin, accent in their speech, or gender*)
3. Primary Source: Copy and distribute Resource Page 4 (TG page 107), Read "Whoopee Ti-Yi-Yo" and discuss answers to the questions.

3. CHECK UNDERSTANDING

Writing   Ask students to write a want ad for a cowboy or cowgirl to work on a cattle drive from San Antonio to Abilene in the 1870s. Be sure to list all the skills—physical and mental—that are necessary for the job.

Thinking About the Chapter (Analyzing)   Engage the class in a discussion of the importance of the railroad and refrigeration to the beef business.

CHAPTER 13 RAILS ACROSS THE COUNTRY

PAGES 58-63

1 Class Period   **Homework: Student Study Guide p. 20**

Chapter Summary

On May 10, 1869, the Central Pacific and Union Pacific lines met, adding new meaning to the name *United* States.

Key Vocabulary

visionaries   subsidy   meridian

1. CONNECT

Remind students of the words "from sea to shining sea" in the song "America the Beautiful." Which two "seas" did the songwriter mean? (*Atlantic and Pacific Oceans*) Ask students to speculate in what ways linking East and West by railroad may have helped to unite the nation after the Civil War.

2. UNDERSTAND

1. Read pages 58-61 through "They did it with incredible speed." Discuss: What hardships and obstacles did the builders of the Central Pacific and Union Pacific have to overcome? (*carry all supplies with them; cut paths through natural barriers; find workers willing to do the hard labor*)
2. Discuss: What role did immigrants and African Americans play in building the railroad? (*Largely Chinese crews laid track for the Central Pacific; Irish immigrants and African Americans worked for the Union Pacific.*)
3. Primary Source: Distribute Resource Page 4 (TG page 107), and read "Drill, Ye Tarriers, Drill." Help students understand that songs like these provided a rhythm and distraction for repetitive work such as that performed by railroad workers.
4. Read the rest of the chapter. Discuss: What legal and illegal methods did railroad owners use to finance construction? (*Legal: government subsidies, sale of stock, low wages. Illegal: crooked contracts, overcharging, unsafe workmanship*)

3. CHECK UNDERSTANDING

Writing   Ask students to write a resume (a list of a person's work experience, skills, and accomplishments) as someone who worked on the Central Pacific or Union Pacific.

Thinking About the Chapter (Evaluating)   Engage students in a discussion of the long-term effects of the transcontinental railroad. (*tied the nation together; speeded transportation of people and goods; made the country seem smaller*)

GEOGRAPHY CONNECTIONS

Have students continue the "Battle for the West" activity described on TG page 46. Referring to the map on page 62 of their books, have students locate and label on their maps the physical features that had to be surmounted in order to lay track linking Sacramento, California and Omaha, Nebraska. Have them label cities along the route.

LINKING DISCIPLINES

Music/History

Play a CD such as *Ken Burns, The West* (PBS) or the soundtrack of *The West* (video, PBS). Discuss the ideas expressed in the songs about work, the West itself, and the historical period in which they were popular.

ACTIVITIES/JOHN HOPKINS TEAM LEARNING

See the Student Team Learning Activity on TG page 55.

READING NONFICTION

Analyzing Word Choice

Discuss how the author creates a setting in which readers can imagine an early train trip west. Have partners begin a word web with the word *adventure* and list words the author uses that are related. Then ask students to refer to their webs and write a sentence telling what the author's feelings are about such a train trip. (*Students should understand that the author thinks the trip was very exciting and novel.*)

GEOGRAPHY CONNECTIONS

Read aloud the passage that ends the chapter on page 67: "But forget the danger and make the trip. You're getting an opportunity that won't last long. You may find it hard to believe, but in a few years this western land will be filled with houses and cities." Refer to Resource Page 5 (TG page 108) and discuss with students the connection between the spread of railroads and the growth of cities.

---

1 Class Period   Homework: Student Study Guide p. 21

Chapter Summary

For passengers, traveling on the transcontinental railroad was one of the great experiences of the late 1800s. But for Plains Indians, the "iron horses" spelled disaster.

Key Vocabulary

transcontinental   emigrant cars
Pullman cars   iron horse

1. CONNECT

Discuss cross-country travel. What are some of the ways people travel from the East Coast to the West Coast? Ask students to estimate how long each method might take.

2. UNDERSTAND

1. Read pages 64-67. Ask a volunteer to read aloud the lines by Walt Whitman on page 64. Discuss: How was the transcontinental railroad like the Northwest Passage sought by Europeans? (*It connected the "Eastern and Western seas," or the Atlantic and Pacific oceans.*)
2. Discuss: How did the emigrant cars and the Pullman cars differ? (*Emigrant cars were low-priced, modest coaches. Pullman cars offered far greater comfort and luxury including beds and meals.*) Look at the pictures of the emigrant car on page 65 and the more elaborate train car at the top of page 66. Ask students which one they would prefer and why.
3. Map: Distribute copies of Resource Page 5 (TG page 114). Discuss the spread of railroads between 1870 and 1890. Ask students how railroads affected the growth of cities (shown in the box on the Resource Page). What other factors besides railroads affected population growth? (*immigration*)

3. CHECK UNDERSTANDING

Writing   Ask students to write a diary entry written by a person traveling by train to Sacramento from Omaha in 1870. Describe the train car, food, and exciting events along the way.

Thinking About the Chapter (Analyzing)   Discuss with students the impact the railroad had on the bison herds on the Great Plains. Have them compare the Buffalo Range shown in the 1850 map on page 83 with the map of the transcontinental railroad on page 62. (*The railroad ran through the buffalo grazing lands, disrupting their habitat and making it possible to shoot them from the train for "sport."*)

CHAPTER 15 — FENCING THE HOMESTEAD

PAGES 68-75

1 Class Period   Homework: Student Study Guide p. 22

Chapter Summary
Once settlers moved into the "Great American Desert," they used technology—windmills, barbed wire, and iron plows—to transform the environment into an agricultural region.

Key Vocabulary
Great American Desert   Grange   barbed wire

1. CONNECT

In this chapter the author says that "the dream of many Americans was to have a farm." Ask students why they think this was the case. (*Having a farm meant being self-sufficient—a farmer could raise animals and crops to feed a family.*)

2. UNDERSTAND

1. Read pages 68-73. Discuss: Why did farmers have a hard time growing crops on the Plains? (*stampeding cattle, few trees, little water, extremes in weather, invasions of grasshoppers, etc.*) Despite these problems, why did so many people head onto the Plains? (*scarce land in the East; the Homestead Act set low prices for public lands in the West*) How did homesteaders solve some of these problems? (*built windmills for water, used barbed wire to fence land*)
2. Map: Have students refer to the map on page 55. Ask: What ended long cattle drives on these trails? (*fenced land, spread of railroads*)
3. Read the last paragraph on page 73 and the first paragraph of the feature. Discuss: How did farming change in the late 1800s? (*became a big business*) According to Willa Cather, what crop became the specialty of many Plains farmers? Why? (*corn, because the climate was right for it*)

3. CHECK UNDERSTANDING

Writing Ask students to imagine they work for Joseph Glidden in the 1870s and write an ad promoting barbed wire. Have them consider these questions before writing: Who are potential customers? How will barbed wire help them?

Thinking About the Chapter (Analyzing) Have students work in teams to list facts supporting the idea that "self-sufficient farming wasn't suited to the Plains." Have them refer to pages 68-74 for details.

GEOGRAPHY CONNECTIONS
Have students continue the "Battle for the West" activity described on TG page 46. Referring to the map on page 75, have students identify and label on their maps the states that were originally covered in whole or in part by tall grass and short grass prairie.

MEETING INDIVIDUAL NEEDS
Some students may be unfamiliar with the farm machinery mentioned in Chapters 15 and 16. Have students pair up to find out more about barbed wire, the steel plow, and McCormick's reaper. A website they can use is *http://memory.loc.gov*, the online Historical Collection of the Library of Congress.

LINKING DISCIPLINES
Art/Geography
Have students use a map of the United States to locate the areas depicted in the three illustrations on pages 70-71. Then ask students to write a short essay comparing and contrasting the two photographs and one painting. Questions to consider: What was the artist or photographer's purpose in creating each of the pieces? What can viewers today learn from each one?

READING NONFICTION

Analyzing Graphic Aids

Have students look at the picture on page 77 and answer this question: If the reaper shown in the picture replaced the hand-held scythe, what invention replaced the horses pulling the reaper?

Analyzing Text Structure

Discuss with students why the author organized the text in this chapter into a cause and effect pattern. (*to point out the effect on farmers, farming, and the land of the invention of the reaper*) Invite partners to create cause and effect chains based on the author's information.

LINKING DISCIPLINES

History/Math

Have students create an example of an installment purchase and calculate interest on the unpaid amount at 18 percent (typical of many credit cards). Then have students list the advantages and disadvantages of installment buying to seller and buyer. (*Advantages—sellers sell more and collect interest from buyers; buyers pay small amounts instead of one big payment. Disadvantages: sellers risk losing money if buyer can't pay; buyers pay interest on the unpaid amount.*)

CHAPTER 16 REAPING A HARVEST
PAGES 76-79

1 Class Period **Homework: Student Study Guide p. 23**

Chapter Summary

The McCormick reaper did for wheat farming what Eli Whitney's cotton gin did for cotton growing. It made big farms practical and profitable.

Key Vocabulary

sod   reaper
scythe   installment buying

1. CONNECT

Unlike 19th-century Americans, many of whom grew the food they ate, Americans today benefit from the agricultural revolution described in this chapter. Ask students where the food they eat comes from. Help them understand that they benefit from the inventions and agricultural research they will learn about in this chapter.

2. UNDERSTAND

1. Read pages 76-78 through "…important part of farming." Discuss: How did Deere's plow and McCormick's reaper revolutionize agriculture? (*plow: provided a way to cut through the tough prairie sod; reaper: speeded up harvest; made big farms practical and profitable*) How did McCormick help expand the Industrial Revolution to agriculture? (*His factories produced farm equipment; installment plan increased demand and speeded the mechanization of agriculture.*)

2. What were some of the negative effects of the farming revolution? (*Small farmers found it difficult to compete; farmers became less self-sufficient and more dependent upon market demand; poor farming methods opened the land to erosion.*)

3. Read the rest of the chapter. Discuss: What actions were taken to counteract the negative effects of the revolution in farming? (*Congress passed the Morrill and Hatch Acts; scientists researched new developments in agriculture.*)

3. CHECK UNDERSTANDING

Writing   Ask students to write the script in Q&A format of an interview with Cyrus McCormick about his business practices as described in Chapter 16.

Thinking About the Chapter (Evaluating)   Have students chart the benefits and costs (pros and cons) of the revolution in agriculture exemplified by the mechanized reaper.

17 THE TRAIL ENDS ON A RESERVATION

PAGES 80-88

1 Class Period   Homework: Student Study Guide p. 24

Chapter Summary

Native Americans found themselves pushed onto unwanted lands called reservations where they were expected to change into farmers or live on government handouts. The 1890 massacre at Wounded Knee marked the end of Native American hopes for autonomy.

1. CONNECT

Read the chapter title and ask students what they think *trail* refers to. Whose trail was it? Where did it lead?

2. UNDERSTAND

1. Read pages 80-82. Discuss: Why couldn't Native Americans and homesteaders exist on the same land? (*Plains Indians were mostly hunters, and needed open land. Homesteaders were farmers or ranchers who needed to fence the land.*)
2. Read pages 83-86. Discuss: Why were Native Americans sent to reservations? (*to move them off land that other Americans wanted; to neutralize them as a threat; to make them dependent and ineffective*) What was the attitude of Sheridan, Pope, and Sherman toward the Native Americans? (*that they should be wiped out*) In what way did the Indian Schools reflect the same goal? (*Their goal was to transform Native Americans into Americans by wiping out their culture.*)
3. Discuss: What are some ways the author suggests the story of Indians and settlers could have been different? (*respect and honesty between Indians and whites, as exemplified in Henry Benjamin Whipple's dealings with Indians; strong laws to prevent unfairness and brutality; better understanding of and caring about other cultures*)

3. CHECK UNDERSTANDING

Writing Ask students to write brief answers to the questions on page 88: "Should [the settlers] have thought of cooperation rather than conquest? Do you think that would have worked?"

Thinking About the Chapter (Making a Time Line) Using the time line on page 88 and information in the books, have students list some of the major events between 1865 and 1890 affecting Native Americans. (*For example, end of Civil War brought a flood of homesteaders onto the Great Plains; completion of transcontinental railroad in 1869 led to destruction of buffalo.*)

GEOGRAPHY CONNECTIONS:

Have students continue the "Battle for the West" activity described on TG page 46. Referring to the map on page 83 of their books, have students identify and mark the approximate extent of the buffalo range in 1850 on their maps. Then have them mark the limit of the buffalo range in 1890, and also the locations and relative sizes of Native American reservations in 1890.

A History of US Sourcebook

1. #61, Chief Joseph (Inmutooyahlatlat), *"I Will Fight No More Forever": Speech to the U.S. Army* (1877)

2. #62, From Chief Joseph (Inmutooyahlatlat), *Address in Washington* (1879)

READING NONFICTION

Analyzing Rhetorical Devices

Have students reread Chief Joseph's quote at the top of page 94 to identify words Chief Joseph uses that stir the listener's sympathy. Ask: What impression does the speaker's voice make in the last *sentence?(The tone is strong, dramatic, and grave.)* Refer to the second quote and ask students to look for a memorable analogy. (*rivers running backward/a man born free and then pent up*) In the last two quotes, have students look for examples of repetition and then discuss how they help the speaker make the point that Indians and whites should be treated the same way.

LINKING DISCIPLINES

Art/History

Have students choose all or part of one of the quotations of Chief Joseph on page 94 (or one from his speeches in *A History of US Sourcebook*). Ask students to copy their quotations onto a sheet of drawing paper and then illustrate it. Collect students' work and display it. Challenge students to memorize the quotation they illustrated, as Joy Hakim suggests.

GEOGRAPHY CONNECTIONS

Have students continue the "Battle for the West" activity described on TG page 46. Referring to the map on page 93, have students locate and mark on their maps the route of the Nez Perce. Have them identify and mark cities, locations, and landforms along the route.

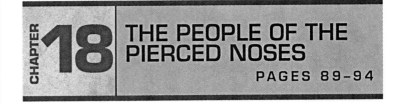

1 Class Period   Homework: Student Study Guide p. 25

Chapter Summary

In one last bid for freedom, Chief Joseph led the Nez Perce on a desperate flight toward Canada. His eloquent appeal for justice on behalf of the Nez Perce confined to reservations has become a rallying cry for people of all races and backgrounds.

Key Vocabulary

rendezvous   bonanza   reservation

1. CONNECT

Have students look at the photograph of Chief Joseph on page 92. At the end of chapter 17, the author refers to him as "a great leader [who] attempted to save his people." Ask students if they have heard of Chief Joseph. Then discuss some of the reasons why this great leader's attempt to save his people is not widely known.

2. UNDERSTAND

1. Read through the third paragraph on page 91. Discuss: What evidence does the author give for her statement that the Nez Perce were special? (*honest, honorable, free-spirited and courageous, intelligent, handsome; lived in a "paradise"*)
2. Read through page 93. Discuss: Why did the flight of Chief Joseph capture so much attention? (*Although outnumbered and outgunned, the Nez Perce—including many women, children, and old people—managed to escape and outwit federal troops several times.*)
3. Read page 94. Have students take turns reading aloud Chief Joseph's words. Discuss: What rights did Chief Joseph demand for his people? (*the right to live as others live; to move about freely; to be subject to the same laws and government as the whites*)

3. CHECK UNDERSTANDING

Writing   Ask students to write a one-paragraph biography of Chief Joseph based on information in the chapter.

Thinking About the Chapter (Analyzing Character)   Engage students in a discussion of Chief Joseph's character. What made him a great leader? How did he show his concern for the people he led? Read aloud his statements on pages 89, 92, and 94. Ask students what picture of a leader emerges from these excerpts.

JOHNS HOPKINS TEAM LEARNING

BEHIND THE HEADLINES

FOCUS ACTIVITY

Ask students to speculate about what revolutions in transportation they will see in their lifetimes. Ask them to imagine how affordable space travel might change their lives.

STUDENT TEAM LEARNING ACTIVITY/RESEARCHING A NEWS STORY

1. Explain that the joining of the two railroads at Promontory, Utah was a great event. Newspaper reporters and telegraph operators spread the news to the folks back east. Divide the class into teams and ask teams to discover the stories behind the following newspaper headlines by reading Chapter 13. Display the following headlines on the chalkboard.

- A Miss and a Hit
- Two Pacifics Meet
- East Races West
- Go Over and Go Under
- A Dollar a Day
- Tycoon or Crook?
- Indians See Red
- A Ten-Day Trip

2. Review or introduce the *Who? What? When? Where? Why?* and *How?* questions for news reports. Ask team members to use this format to record facts for each of the headlines. (Teams should assign specific headlines to their members.)

3. **Circulate and Monitor** Visit each team while the students read the chapter to help them locate and record information.

4. Using **Numbered Heads,** have teams share the story behind each headline.

SUMMARIZING PART 3

NOTE FROM THE AUTHOR

I like to ask children to write their own tests. They have to think to do that. Then I have them answer their own questions and someone else's as well.

USING THE RUBRICS

To assess these writing assignments, group projects, and activities, scoring rubrics have been provided at the back of this Teaching Guide. Be sure to explain the rubrics to your students.

ASSESSMENT

Part 3 Check-Up   Use Check-Up 3 (TG page 99) to assess student learning in Part 3.

ALTERNATE ASSESSMENT

Ask students to write an essay answering one of the following questions, which link the big ideas across chapters:

1. Making Connections   How did the growth of the railroad help end the way of life for Native Americans on the Plains? (*It led to the sale of Native American land, destruction of the buffalo, and the flood of homesteaders onto the Plains.*)

2. Making Connections   How did the spread of the Industrial Revolution onto the Plains change farming in the United States? (*The use of farm machinery required capital, which in turn helped make farming into a big business.*)

DEBATING THE ISSUES

Use the topic below to stimulate debate.

Resolved   That Native Americans after the Civil War should fight for control of their land regardless of the consequences. (On page 82 the author asks students if they would be willing to leave their homes for a reservation. Ask some students to act as U.S. Commissioners sent to talk Native Americans into resettling on reservations. Others should imagine they are members of a Native American council who must debate the proposals.)

MAKING ETHICAL JUDGMENTS

The following questions ask students to consider issues of ethics.

1. On page 85, the author explores what happens when one group of people have a home and another group either wants that home or has no home at all. Is there any way people can share their resources so that everybody has a place to live? These are tough questions. First, consider the Native Americans. Land in the East was becoming scarce. Does that mean that the government was justified in taking Native American land on the Plains? Then, what about the homeless today? Does society, or the community, have a responsibility to care for them? Why or why not?

2. On page 88 the author asks whether readers think modern industrial cultures have a duty to protect native peoples and their natural environments. Or should the native cultures be forced to learn new ways of life? (*Review the changes forced upon Native Americans. Next, focus on a native culture resisting changes today—Native people in the Amazon rain forests, the Masai on the savannas of East Africa, the nomads of Tibet. Are modern cultures helping or hurting by trying to teach people of ancient cultures new ways of living?*)

PROJECTS AND ACTIVITIES

Writing a Ballad   Tell students that cowhands kept cattle from stampeding by singing ballads. Challenge students to write a "cattle lullaby" that captures life on the trail. If possible, have students locate some ballads to play in class.

Using Historical Imagination   Divide the class into four groups. Have each group devise a story that one of the following people might tell a grandchild about the first transcontinental railroad: (a) a Chinese railroad worker, (b) an Irish railroad worker, (c) a Cheyenne who saw the first "iron horse," (d) an Easterner who took one of the first transcontinental trips aboard an "emigrant car."

Writing Poetry   Review the Stephen Vincent Benét poem on page 70. Then challenge students to write their own poems about homesteading. Tell students to use at least three of the following words in their poems: *sod, buffalo grass, grasshoppers, blizzard, drought, buffalo, prairie dog, tornado, prairie, brush fire, pioneer.*

Designing an Advertisement   Have students draw poster-sized advertisements for the McCormick reaper. Ads should describe advantages of the reaper and methods of payment. Remind students that the installment plan was just as new as the reaper.

Interpreting a Map   Refer students to the map on page 83 and help them understand that all of the ceded land shown was occupied by Native Americans before the 1860s. Have them compare that amount of Native American land with the amount occupied by Native Americans in 1890. Challenge students to estimate the percentage of land lost. Have students refer to the text to find reasons for this great change.

Doing Library Research   Ask volunteers to take the author's suggestion on page 89. Have them research the lives of Crazy Horse, Sitting Bull, Black Hawk, and Geronimo, as well as other leading Native Americans such as Red Cloud. You might have students present their findings in the form of autobiographical monologues for the class.

Investigative Reports-   Divide students into small groups of newspaper reporters, each assigned to cover the completion of the Transcontinental Railroad. Tell the students that a source has accused both Leland Stanford and Thomas Durant of unfair business practices, and that it is their job to uncover more about these two men to get to the truth. Have each group choose one of the men and research their background and accomplishments. Have them write an objective newspaper editorial, describing either Stanford or Durant's life and accomplishments, and determining the balance between the good and bad they caused.

Analyzing Primary Sources

Tell students that in 1890 the Superintendent of the U.S. Census made this announcement:

> *Up to and including 1880, the country had a frontier of settlement, but at present the unsettled area has been so broken into...that there can hardly be said to be a frontier line....[W]estward movement...cannot, therefore, any longer have a place in the census reports.*

What change did the Superintendent declare? *(closing of the frontier)* Do students think this means that there were no more new frontiers for Americans to cross? *(Lead students to understand that frontier can refer to any groundbreaking endeavor.)* Explain that Part 4 gives students their first look at a chronological frontier—the closing years of the 19th century. Ask students how they feel about taking part in the beginning of a new century.

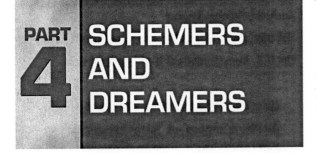

PART 4 SCHEMERS AND DREAMERS

THE BIG IDEAS

In the late 1800s, many of the nation's large cities belonged to political bosses. Bosses held onto power because they made it their business to know people's needs and to tend to the problems of everyday life. Explained Martin Lomasney, boss of Boston's South End:

There's got to be in every ward somebody that any bloke can come to—no matter what he's done—and get help. Help, you understand, none of your law and justice, but help.

The corruption and hucksterism of the era led authors Mark Twain and Charles Dudley Warner to call the times the Gilded Age. Part 4 traces changes at the end of the Civil War that gave rise to the schemers and the dreamers of the last three decades of the century. It also looks at efforts to promote reform by exposing the injustices of political corruption.

INTRODUCING PART 4

SETTING GOALS

Introduce Part 4 by writing *circus* on the chalkboard. Ask the class to suggest images the word suggests: trained animals; three rings of action; variety; thrills; clowns and excitement. Explain that in Part 4 they will meet P. T. Barnum, whose circus, "The Greatest Show on Earth" was famous in the 19th century. They'll also learn about the "circus" of politics in the Gilded Age.

To set goals for Part 4, tell students that they will
- describe the problems of pollution in American cities in the 19th century.
- understand the tone and conduct of politics in the Gilded Age.
- assess the greatness of Mark Twain.

SETTING A CONTEXT FOR READING

Thinking About the Big Ideas   You might open Part 4 by asking students the question raised by the author on page 95: Do you ever worry about air pollution or dishonest politicians? Then tell students that these issues also concerned people in the late 1800s. As students read Part 4, have them write down reasons pollution and corruption were problems at this time. To connect past with present, students should note changes that have eliminated or lessened these problems.

Identifying Author's Viewpoint   In Chapters 19-21 author Joy Hakim introduces "schemers, dreamers, and villains" and clearly indicates her opinion about them. Ask students to look for clues about the author's viewpoint. They can make individual charts with these headings: *Person, Author's Opinion,* and *My Opinion.* Have them use the chart to cite specific examples of the author's viewpoint (and their own) as they read Part 4.

SETTING A CONTEXT IN SPACE AND TIME

Connecting Demographics and Geography In the late 1800s, the landscape of America began to change as the urban population started to grow by leaps and bounds. To illustrate this change, have students study the "Population of Major Cities" maps and tables in the Atlas of their books. Then, copy the following statistics onto the chalkboard:

Rural Population
1870: 28,625,000
1880: 36,026,000
1890: 40,873,000
1900: 45,835,000

Urban Population
1870: 9,902,000
1880: 14,130,000
1890: 22,106,000
1900: 30,160,000

Have students use these figures in a line graph. Then ask: Which label best describes the United States at the end of Reconstruction—urban or rural? (*rural*) Which part of the population grew the fastest at the end of the 1800s? (*urban*) Which regions of the country experienced the most rapid growth? In which regions did the least population growth occur? Have students compare the national rate of population growth between 1860 and 1890 to regional growth to draw conclusions about migrations that occurred. (*out of the South and Northeast and into the Midwest and West*) Challenge students to speculate on some of the problems rapid urban growth might cause. Use this activity to lead into Chapter 19.

Understanding Change Over Time Begin Part 4 by asking students to define the term *age*. Some students might mention chronological age; others might talk about a specific stage of life, such as old age. Tell students that the term also refers to a historical period characterized or strongly influenced by some feature or person. Challenge students to brainstorm the names of some historical ages. (*Examples: Ice Age, Elizabethan Age, Space Age, Jazz Age*) Then tell students that Part 4 takes a look at another historical age—the Gilded Age. Ask them to imagine what that name implies.

READING NONFICTION

Analyzing Graphic Devices

The cartoons in Chapter 19 are judgments of Boss Tweed made by cartoonist Thomas Nast. Without having read anything about Tweed, what would the cartoon on page 95 tell you? (*The "money bag" face says he is rich; the fat belly says he is self-indulgent.*)

MEETING INDIVIDUAL NEEDS

Have students keep an index card file of the cast of characters in Part 4. Each card should contain the name and a brief description of the person. For example, Boss Tweed, corrupt politician in New York City; Thomas Nast, cartoonist, attacked Boss Tweed by making fun of him in cartoons that appeared in newspapers; Alfred Ely Beach, inventor of a New York subway that was never built. Students can add cards as they read Chapters 20 and 21.

1 Class Period   Homework: Student Study Guide p. 26

Chapter Summary

Bosses such as William Marcy Tweed built political machines that lay outside the system of checks and balances set up by the Constitution. Nonetheless, they found themselves checked by yet another nongovernmental power—the scathing pen of political cartoonist Thomas Nast.

Key Vocabulary

Tammany Hall	scoundrel	subway
political machine	graft	constituent

1. CONNECT

Ask students to list the ways we get news about politicians today. (*newspapers, TV and radio, Internet, magazines*) In the 1870s, how did people get news? (*newspapers*) Explain that newspapers were the main source of news.

2. UNDERSTAND

1. Read pages 95-97. Discuss: Why was pollution a problem in large cities such as New York? (*crowded living conditions, many horses, coal used for fuel, oil refineries, limited sanitary services*)
2. Discuss: What is a "political machine"? (*an unofficial local government, offering services to people at a price*) How did Boss Tweed build one? (*took control of jobs and services, bribed officials, offered immigrants help in exchange for votes*)
3. Read the rest of the chapter. Discuss: How did Alfred Ely Beach and Thomas Nast challenge Tweed's power? (*Beach: built a subway without Tweed's knowledge; Nast: exposed and ridiculed Tweed in political cartoons*)

3. CHECK UNDERSTANDING

Writing   Write a postcard to a friend in the West describing your visit to New York City in 1870. Be sure to mention the pollution and your ride on Beach's subway.

Thinking About the Chapter (Analyzing)   For each of Thomas Nast's cartoons in the chapter, have students answer the following questions: What is going on in the cartoon? Who is being depicted? What is the overall message?

20 PHINEAS TAYLOR BARNUM

PAGES 101–104

1 Class Period   Homework: Student Study Guide p. 27

Chapter Summary

"There's a sucker born every minute," is a saying people attribute to P. T. Barnum. Americans so enjoyed Barnum's form of hucksterism that he turned his Barnum and Bailey Circus into "The Greatest Show on Earth."

Key Vocabulary

humbug   huckster   prohibition

1. CONNECT

Ask students to imagine that they live in a world without modern entertainment devices. Ask: What you would do for entertainment? (*get together with friends, sing, play music and games, tell stories, go for walks*) That's what people in the 19th century did. Have students volunteer to give up all their modern amusements and find other forms of entertainment, and then report back about what they did.

2. UNDERSTAND

1. Read the chapter. Discuss: What did P. T. Barnum mean when he called himself the Prince of Humbug? (*that he excelled at fooling people*) Why didn't people seem to mind being tricked by Barnum? (*because he made them laugh*)
2. Discuss: How did Barnum fit the age in which he lived? (*He combined extremes—a desire for money with a desire to do good.*)

3. CHECK UNDERSTANDING

Writing   Ask students to create the text for a poster announcing the arrival of P. T. Barnum's "Greatest Show on Earth," using specific information from Chapter 20.

Thinking About the Chapter (Analyzing)   Have students discuss the role of railroads in the success of Barnum's circus.

READING NONFICTION

Analyzing Point of View

Have students discuss why the author included P. T. Barnum in Book Seven. Is it because he was a skilled promoter who represents the extremes of the Gilded Age? From the author's point of view, what other significance did "The Greatest Show on Earth" have? (*The circus brought people together; gave city dwellers and farmers, immigrants and native-born, something in common, a shared "all-American" experience.*)

LINKING DISCIPLINES

Music/History

Play a selection of songs from the 1880s and 1890s and discuss how they reflect the Gilded Age and differ from popular songs today.

ACTIVITIES/JOHNS HOPKINS TEAM LEARNING

See the Team Learning Activity on TG page 63. Use this activity for reading Chapters 20 and 21.

Have students locate the Mississippi River on a map of the United States. Assign a team of students to find out about the use of the river today. Is it still as important for commerce and passenger travel as it was when Mark Twain was writing?

CHAPTER 21

HUCK, TOM, AND FRIENDS

PAGES 105-110

1 Class Period   Homework: Student Study Guide p. 28

Chapter Summary

In vivid prose, Mark Twain captured the dreams, schemes, and hopes of a people as he described everyday life in the closing years of the 19th century.

Key Vocabulary

Gilded Age   sumptuous
exigencies   apprentice

1. CONNECT

Bring some of your favorite books to class. Make a class list of favorite books for the beach, a long car trip, or for a desert island. Then introduce Tom and Huck by reading aloud excerpts from *Tom Sawyer* or *Huckleberry Finn*.

2. UNDERSTAND

1. Read pages 105-108. Discuss the author's question: What similarities are there in the life stories of Ben Franklin and Samuel Clemens? (*Both learned printing by working for their older brothers. Neither liked being bossed around, so they left to take printing and writing jobs elsewhere.*)
2. Read the rest of the chapter. Discuss: How did Mark Twain view the Gilded Age? (*as a time of "ridiculous excess"*)
3. Map: Have students use a map of the United States to track the travels of Sam Clemens described in the chapter. Ask them to start at Hannibal, Missouri, where he grew up.

3. CHECK UNDERSTANDING

Writing   Ask students to choose a quote of Mark Twain's from the chapter and write an essay, poem, or story using the quote as a starting point.

Thinking About the Chapter (Hypothesizing)   Ask students to imagine what Twain would say about the United States today. Would he see this as another Gilded Age of "ridiculous excess"? Would he see this as a nation that has forgotten its ideals? Have students give some examples that support their answers.

JOHNS HOPKINS TEAM LEARNING

PHINEAS T. BARNUM AND MARK TWAIN

1 CLASS PERIOD

FOCUS ACTIVITY

1. Bring to class a sufficient number of business cards so that students working in pairs can consider two or three examples. Discuss the purpose of business cards and with the students list on the chalkboard categories of information that might appear on a business card. For example:
- the name of the person and his or her profession or business
- accomplishments or facts about the person and his profession or business
- logo or slogan
- quotation

2. Then divide the class into pairs and provide each pair with two or more samples of business cards. Ask students to evaluate the design and information on the cards to determine how well they achieve their purpose.

STUDENT TEAM LEARNING ACTIVITY/ORGANIZING BIOGRAPHICAL INFORMATION

1. Have students **Partner Read** Chapter 20 to describe P. T. Barnum and his amazing entertainments.

2. Following the reading, have students work in teams. Use **Roundtable** and a sheet of chart paper to record words and phrases that describe Barnum, his great showmanship, and his accomplishments. Use **Think-Team-Share** to discuss why *Life* magazine chose Barnum as one of the hundred most important people of the millennium and described him as the "patron saint of promoters."

3. Then have students **Partner Read** Chapter 21 to describe Twain and his accomplishments as a humorist and author.

4. Following the reading, ask teams to use **Roundtable** and a sheet of chart paper to record words and phrases that describe Twain, his accomplishments as a writer and humorist and his adventures as a world traveler. Ask students to use **Think-Team-Share** to discuss the question: Why is Twain's writing important? (*Twain used humor to say something important and serious; celebrated American life but reminded readers that the promises of America, such as freedom and opportunity for all, were not being met; coined the term* Gilded Age *to explain the ridiculous excesses of his times.*)

5. Distribute unlined index cards to each team and ask each team to design two business cards: one for Barnum and one for Twain. Help students decide what information might appear on the business cards by referring them back to the sample cards they analyzed earlier.

6. Sharing Information   Ask teams to display their Barnum and Twain business cards and explain their choices of wording and design.

SUMMARIZING PART 4

ASSESSMENT

Part 4 Check-Up   Use Check-Up 4 (TG page 100) to assess student learning in Part 4.

ALTERNATE ASSESSMENT
Ask students to write an essay answering the following question, which links the big ideas across chapters.

Making Connections   Imagine that you live in the late 1800s. You have read Shakespeare's description (see page 108) of a gilded age. Do you agree that the description fits the age in which you live? Why or why not? (*Most students will probably agree, citing the corruption and lavish spending of a Boss Tweed or the hucksterism and generosity of a P.T. Barnum.*)

USING THE RUBRICS

To assess these writing assignments, group projects, and activities, scoring rubrics have been provided at the back of this Teaching Guide. Be sure to explain the rubrics to your students.

DEBATING THE ISSUES
Use the topic below to stimulate debate.

Resolved   That political machines should be outlawed as unconstitutional. (Appoint some students to speak for pro-machine politicians such as George Washington Plunkitt. Have others speak from the point of view of immigrants who have been helped by the political bosses. Instruct yet other students to represent reformers such as Thomas Nast and Alfred Ely Beach.)

MAKING ETHICAL JUDGMENTS
The following question asks students to consider issues of ethics.

In the caption for the Boss Tweed cartoon on page 95, Thomas Nast asks: "Well, what are you going to do about it?" If you were a voter in New York City in the 1870s, how would you answer that question? (*Encourage students to think of ways that citizens can influence political processes—e.g., write letters to honest legislators demanding an investigation, work to elect anticorruption city officials, write letters to the editor, and so on.*)

PROJECTS AND ACTIVITIES
Writing Captions   Refer students to the political cartoon on page 96. Working individually or in small groups, students can write captions expressing the cartoon's message. From these captions, ask students what they can infer about one of the ways in which the Tammany machine built its power. (*by paying people for do-nothing jobs*)

Writing an Obituary   Ask students to imagine they are reporters for a New York newspaper and have them write an obituary for Alfred Ely Beach. The columns should profile Beach's lifetime achievements, including his role in promoting justice. (If students aren't sure what an obituary includes, supply examples from your local paper.)

Designing an Advertisement Have students work in small groups to design posters announcing the arrival of the Barnum and Bailey Circus in a small town on the Midwest prairie. Posters should highlight the attractions of the three-ring circus.

Making Oral Book Reports Ask interested students to read a book or short stories written by Mark Twain. Have them present the plots to the class in the form of a storytelling session.

LOOKING AHEAD

Developing Empathy

In 1894, a young Russian Jewish girl named Mary Antin recalled her parents' decision to go to America:

> So at last I was going to America! The boundaries burst. The arch of heaven soared. A million suns shone out for every star. The winds rushed in from outer space, roaring in my ears, "America! America!"

Explain that Part 5 introduces some of the people who came to the United States in the late nineteenth century seeking the "promised land."

IN SEARCH OF LIBERTY

THE BIG IDEAS

In 1884, the Statue of Liberty arrived in New York Harbor. The gift from France lacked a pedestal, so Hungarian immigrant Joseph Pulitzer used his newspaper to raise the money. Some 120,000 Americans sent in a small fortune in dimes and nickels. In 1886, when the city set the statue in place, an American Jew named Emma Lazarus donated a poem for its base. Here are those now-famous lines:

Give me your tired, your poor,
Your huddled masses yearning to breathe free,
The wretched refuse of your teeming shore,
Send these, the homeless, tempest-tost, to me:
I lift my lamp beside the golden door…

The diversity of people who helped raise the Statue of Liberty was rivaled only by the diversity of immigrants who arrived in the United States in the late 1800s. Nearly all came in search of freedom—economic, political, and religious. Part 5 explores the nation's growing diversity and efforts of reformers to win greater justice for all.

INTRODUCING PART 5

SETTING GOALS

Introduce Part 5 by discussing the Part title. Ask students to define *liberty*. (*freedom*) Remind students that in the Declaration of Independence liberty is linked with "life" and the "pursuit of happiness" as the three unalienable human rights. Then ask a volunteer to read aloud the titles of Chapters 22-28. Ask students to speculate why immigrants and women were searching for liberty in the United States after the Civil War. (*Immigrants were not free in their own countries; women could not vote in this country.*)

To set goals for Part 5, tell students that they will
• describe reasons immigrants came to the United States.
• identify achievements of some immigrants.
• chart opposition to immigration.
• track the consequences of anti-Chinese racism.
• identify issues behind the campaign for women's suffrage.

SETTING A CONTEXT FOR READING

Thinking About the Big Ideas To introduce the concept of diversity, tell students that the United States is like a "mini-United Nations." Ask what this means. (*People from all over the world live here.*) Ask volunteers to identify their national, ethnic, or regional ancestry, and list responses on the chalkboard. During Part 5, have students identify which of the groups listed arrived in large numbers during the late 1800s. Call on volunteers to investigate the peak years for other groups not covered in Part 5.

Identifying Cause and Effect   In Chapters 22-28, Joy Hakim provides information for comparing and contrasting attitudes of immigrants and those who opposed immigration; the ideals of the U.S. Constitution and the campaign for women's suffrage. Encourage students to note and discuss these connections as they read through the chapters.

SETTING A CONTEXT IN SPACE AND TIME

Using Maps   To help students envision immigration to the United States during the late 1800s, refer them to the map on page 114. Ask them to identify the three regions that sent the largest number of immigrants. (*northern Europe, central Europe, southern Europe*) From this map, what can students infer about changes in U.S. population during these years? (*It was growing and becoming more diverse.*)

Understanding Change Over Time   To help students understand changing immigration patterns, refer them to the graph on page 114. Ask them in which years immigration was lowest. (*1861-1862 and 1880*) What historic events accounted for this? (*Civil War and a depression*) In which decade did immigration peak? (*1880s*) Tell students that in Part 5 they will learn why so many immigrants came to the United States at that time.

Analyzing Text Features

Reread the chapter title, and ask partners to skim the chapter to find the different ways the author has organized the text in order to let "immigrants speak." Have partners identify text features, such as sidebars and shaded and italicized blocks of text, that present primary sources and also find direct quotes cited within the text. Then discuss: Why does the author present these primary sources? (*to help readers understand the immigrants' experiences first-hand*)

LINKING DISCIPLINES

Math/Social Studies

Have students make a bar graph based on the information on the map on page 114. The graph will show how many people came to the United States from different parts of the world between 1860 and 1900.

GEOGRAPHY CONNECTIONS

Have students use the graph on page 114 to pose and answer questions about the effect of events on the geographic patterns of immigration. Ask them to speculate about the following: The regions or nations that experienced the greatest decrease in numbers of immigrants following 1882. The effect of the Civil War and the depression on the number of European immigrants. The years that the greatest number of Europeans probably arrived.

CHAPTER 22 IMMIGRANTS SPEAK

PAGES 111–118

1 Class Period   Homework: Student Study Guide p. 29

Chapter Summary

Although the Germans and Irish made up the largest groups of 19th-century immigrants, the late 1800s saw a flood of newcomers from eastern and southern Europe. Their arrival fueled the growth of cities and industry, propelling the nation into the modern era.

Key Vocabulary

immigrate	emigrate	tenements
steerage a	bysmal	

1. CONNECT

On the chalkboard, write *opportunity* and discuss its meaning. (*chance for a desirable outcome*). Discuss why America was (and still is) seen as the "land of opportunity."

2. UNDERSTAND

1. Read pages 111-113, through paragraph three. Discuss: Why would John Smith have welcomed the immigrants who came in the 19th century? (*They had the skills to build, farm, and invent.*) What opportunities did Carl Schurz find that helped him become a leader? (*studied law, served in politics, had careers in government, the military, and journalism*)

2. Read the rest of the chapter. Discuss: Why did immigrants come to America during the second half of the 19th century? (*to escape political unrest, famine, lack of work, and religious persecution, and to find economic security*)

3. Chart: Have each student make a chart showing the nationalities of immigrants introduced in Chapters 22, 23, and 28. Use the following headings: *Name; Reason for Coming (if known), Contribution to U.S.*

3. CHECK UNDERSTANDING

Writing   Ask students to think about what is going on and what is at stake for the boys in the photograph on page 115. Then ask them to write a caption from the boys' point of view.

Thinking About the Chapter (Identifying Main Idea)   Discuss the author's question: Do you know what Carl Schurz meant when he said, "Equality of rights…is the great moral element of a true democracy"? To kick off discussion, repeat a quote by Frederick Douglass: "No man can put a chain about the ankle of his fellow man without at last finding the other end fastened about his own neck."

CHAPTER 23

MORE ABOUT IMMIGRANTS

PAGES 119–122

1 Class Period   Homework: Student Study Guide p. 30

Chapter Summary

Although most immigrants cherished American ideals, not all Americans welcomed them. The backlash against immigrants took the form of ugly ethnic, racial, and religious prejudice.

Key Vocabulary

prejudice   Know-Nothings
racism   anti-Semitic

1. CONNECT

Discuss: Why would some people in the 19th century have opposed immigration? (*competition for jobs; prejudice against people who are different from themselves; racism*) Why do some people today want to limit legal immigration? (*for the same reasons*)

2. UNDERSTAND

1. Read the chapter. Tell students that members of the Know-Nothing party used the name to conceal their activities— i.e., "we know nothing." In reality they did know nothing about the talents and cultures of immigrants.
2. Discuss: What values did Chinese immigrants have? (*honesty, fairness, and loyalty; a balanced life; respect for learning and family*) Why were they unwelcome? (*In a depression, the Chinese worked for low wages. Untrue stories about them and their different appearance led to racism.*)
3. Primary Source: Distribute Resource Page 6 (TG page 109). Point out that while the Chinese Exclusion act was supposed to expire in ten years, it kept being renewed until it became permanent. It was finally repealed in 1943 because by then there were other restrictions on Asian immigrants.

3. CHECK UNDERSTANDING

Writing   Ask students to write a letter to the editor of a newspaper in 1882, protesting the Chinese Exclusion Act. Encourage them to use information about Chinese contributions to the building of the transcontinental railroad along with other arguments.

Thinking About the Chapter (Synthesizing)   Discuss how the prejudice and violent actions of the Know-Nothing Party, the Ku Klux Klan, and the Workingman's Party might have led to passage of the Chinese Exclusion Act.

READING NONFICTION
Analyzing Word Choice

After reading through page 120, review with students the definitions of *bias* and *prejudice*. Ask individual students to list words the author uses to describe bias and prejudice, and the bias some Americans had against immigrants in general and Chinese immigrants in particular. Then ask students to write a sentence describing the writer's judgment of people who were prejudiced.

LINKING DISCIPLINES
Math/Social Studies

Have students do the calculation to answer the author's question on page 120: What percentage of the total U.S. population in 1882 was Chinese? (*0.06 percent; the population of the United States was 50,000,000; of whom 300,000 had emigrated from China.*)

MEETING INDIVIDUAL NEEDS

Some students will benefit from referring to a world map (such as the one in the Atlas) to trace the route by which most Chinese immigrants came to the United States (crossing the Pacific Ocean and landing in California).

LINKING DISCIPLINES

History/Art

Have students look at the illustration at the top of page 125 and infer the artist's point of view. Ask them to look carefully at what is going on in the picture. Is the violence one-sided? What is happening to the three Chinese men in the foreground? How many men are attacking them? What are the men with hats in the center of the picture doing? Ask students to consider this picture in light of the Chinese Exclusion Act. Discuss: Who is destroying property in the picture? Who do you think took the blame for the destruction of property? Do you think the artist supported the Chinese Exclusion Act? Why? Ask students to write a caption for the picture based on their understanding of prejudice against the Chinese.

1 Class Period   Homework: Student Study Guide p. 31

Chapter Summary

The Chinese of San Francisco felt the lash of prejudice when white law officials shut down their laundries. The fact that white-owned laundries remained open added extra sting to the injustice.

Key Vocabulary

ordinance   naturalized citizen
nativism   Chinese Exclusion Act

1. CONNECT

Write *citizenship* on the chalkboard, and discuss what it means to be a U.S. citizen. How does a person become a citizen? (*by being born in the U.S. or by being naturalized—made a citizen by law*) What right does the Constitution reserve for a citizen by birth and denies to a naturalized citizen? (*Article II, Section 5 of the Constitution states that the President must be a citizen by birth.*)

2. UNDERSTAND

1. Read the chapter. Discuss: Why did many Chinese immigrants set up laundries and restaurants in mining towns? (*Starting a laundry required little capital and American and European men thought washing and cooking was "women's work."*) How did racism play a part in San Francisco's decision to shut down laundries in wooden buildings? (*Officials applied the ordinance only to Chinese laundries.*)
2. Discuss the author's question: "When officials shut down a laundry owned by a woman, what kind of prejudice was that?" (*sexism*)

3. CHECK UNDERSTANDING

Writing Ask students to write a paragraph explaining how a person from another country can become a citizen today.

Thinking About the Chapter (Hypothesizing) Ask students to consider the author's statement, "If you want to understand history, take yourself to past times." Discuss some of the ways you can "take yourself to past times." Define some other ways of understanding history.

25 GOING TO COURT

PAGES 126-129

1 Class Period   Homework: Student Study Guide p. 31

Chapter Summary

The case of *Yick Wo* v. *Hopkins* revealed the power of the 14th Amendment. In a landmark decision, the Supreme Court used the equal protection clause to overturn the decision to shut down Chinese laundries in San Francisco.

Key Vocabulary

appeal	criminal law	civil law
aliens	defendant	prosecutors

1. CONNECT

Discuss the meaning of "have your day in court." *(having a chance to stand up for your rights by being heard in court)* Ask students to review the situation in which Lee Yick found himself in 1886. Explain that this chapter tells the outcome of the case.

2. UNDERSTAND

1. Read the chapter. Discuss: What was the central question in the case of *Yick Wo* v. *Hopkins?* (*Did a Chinese immigrant such as Lee Yick have the same rights as if he were an American citizen?*)
2. Ask: What types of law cases exist in the United States? (*civil and criminal*) How do they differ? (*In a civil case, no criminal laws have been broken.*) What type of case was *Yick Wo?* Why? (*a criminal case, because a San Francisco criminal law had been broken*) Why was the *Yick Wo* case so important? (*It considered the right of police to enforce a law arbitrarily. It also decided whether aliens had the same rights as citizens.*) What was the Supreme Court's ruling? (*The Court ruled that the polices' actions violated the equal protection clause of the 14th Amendment.*)

3. CHECK UNDERSTANDING

Writing   Ask students to write a letter to students at the Yick Wo Elementary School in San Francisco introducing Lee Yick and explaining the significance of the name of their school.

Thinking About the Chapter (Evaluating)   Discuss the reason the author says the decision in *Yick Wo* v. *Hopkins* was momentous.

READING NONFICTION

Analyzing Text Organization

Discuss with students the author's twofold purpose in organizing information about the law and the case *Yick Wo* v. *Hopkins* in a chronological pattern. (*The author not only wants readers to understand that sequence of events and the outcome that occurred in the case Yick Wo v. Hopkins but to understand the step-by-step process of the U.S. legal system.*)

HISTORY ARCHIVES

A History of US Sourcebook

#63, Stanley Matthews, *Opinion in Yick Wo v. Hopkins, Sheriff, etc.* (1886)

ACTIVITIES/JOHNS HOPKINS TEAM LEARNING

See the Team Learning Activity on TG page 75.

CHAPTER 26

TEA IN WYOMING

PAGES 130–132

LINKING DISCIPLINES

Art/Language Arts

Read the extended metaphor on page 132, paragraph 2: "It's kind of a wild ride on a single track...giddy girls at the brakes." Discuss whether the "mythical railroad man" who reportedly said this was for or against women's suffrage in Wyoming. Then have students create a pro-women's suffrage cartoon using the image of a train to stand for women's suffrage and a strong pro-suffrage caption, such as "We won't be sidetracked [pulled off the main track to let a faster train go by] in our journey to suffrage!"

1 Class Period   **Homework: Student Study Guide p. 32**

Chapter Summary

Wyoming led the way in granting the vote to women. When the United States threatened to deny the territory statehood unless it abandoned women's suffrage, a representative declared: "We may stay out of the Union a hundred years, but we will come in with our women."

Key Vocabulary

suffrage   veto   justice of the peace

1. CONNECT

Have each student choose a number between 1 and 10 and display the number. Next, ask them to vote on an issue affecting the whole class...but, only those students with odd numbers can vote. Ask the "evens" how it feels to be excluded.

2. UNDERSTAND

1. Read the chapter. Discuss: What public office did Esther Morris hold before women could vote? (*justice of the peace*) What role did she play in the suffrage movement? (*She convinced Wyoming legislators to back a women's suffrage bill.*) How did women's suffrage in Wyoming Territory affect the nation when Wyoming became a state? (*Admission of Wyoming as a state with women's suffrage allowed women to vote in national elections.*)

2. Map: Have students complete Resource Page 7 (TG page 110) to learn more about the advance of women's suffrage.

3. CHECK UNDERSTANDING

Writing   Ask students to take the part of a newspaper reporter and write a list of questions they would ask in an interview with Esther Morris.

Thinking About the Chapter (Analyzing)   Discuss the fears men and women expressed about women's suffrage. What did they think would happen? What actually happened in Wyoming?

27 ARE YOU A CITIZEN IF YOU CAN'T VOTE?

PAGES 133-139

1 Class Period   Homework: Student Study Guide p. 32

Chapter Summary

In the struggle for women's suffrage, leaders such as Susan B. Anthony risked arrest and trial for casting trial ballots. Others, such as Belva Lockwood, pushed themselves into law practice so they could defend women's rights more forcefully.

Key Vocabulary

temperance   benign

1. CONNECT

Discuss the question in the title of this chapter. (*The answer is "yes." For example, young people under age 18 are citizens, but they cannot vote.*) Discuss the restated question: "Are you an adult citizen if you can't vote?"

2. UNDERSTAND

1. Read pages 133-135, up to the last paragraph. Discuss: What legal injustices faced women in the late 1800s? (*They could be taxed, but could not vote; they could be arrested, but couldn't serve on a jury.*)
2. Read the rest of the chapter. Discuss: What was the main question raised in the trial of Susan B. Anthony? (*If women are citizens, why don't they have the right to vote?*) Refer students back to page 134 and read aloud the provisions of the 15th Amendment. Ask: What new issue did the trial raise? (*the right to a free trial in a free society*) Discuss the author's question: Was John Adams right in his predictions cited on page 139? (*Students can refer to the Constitution for amendments that expanded suffrage.*)

3. CHECK UNDERSTANDING

Writing   Have students write a newspaper editorial answering some of the objections to women's suffrage posed by men and women.

Thinking About the Chapter (Making Inferences)   Engage students in a discussion of the ways in which women's suffrage exemplified the sprit of the second half of the 19th century: expansion of opportunities; inventions that moved people along quickly: train, bicycle; the wide open spaces.

READING NONFICTION

Analyzing Point of View

Ask students to reiterate Susan Anthony's view on women's right to vote. (*Women should have the right.*) Read Anthony's quote from page 138, "We, the people does not mean We, the male citizens." Ask: Does Anthony use logic or appeal to the emotions to persuade people of her view? (*logic*) Students can find out more about women's suffrage at the National Archives and Records Administration website: www.nara.gov/education/teaching/woman/home.html

HISTORY ARCHIVES

A History of US Sourcebook
#58, Susan B. Anthony, *"Are Women Persons?":*
Address after Her Arrest for Illegal Voting (1873)

1 Class Period   Homework: Student Study Guide p. 33

Chapter Summary

In her autobiography, Mary Antin gave a voice to the hopes, hardships, and dreams of many immigrants. For Antin, the United States was indeed *The Promised Land.*

Key Vocabulary

beyond the pale   *shtetl*   *rebbe*

1. CONNECT

Remind students that there are some places in the world that do not have free public education. Explain that in the 19th century education for all was not available anywhere else in the world besides the United States. A free education continues to be one of the opportunities that pull immigrants to the United States.

2. UNDERSTAND

1. Read pages 140-145 aloud, with students taking turns reading the selections from Mary Antin's autobiography. Discuss: Why did Antin's family leave Russia? (*to escape the poverty and lack of liberty born of religious prejudice*) What aspects of American life most pleased the Antins? (*right to a free public education; right to live, travel, and work wherever they wanted; the freedom of speech and religion*)

2. Distribute Resource Page 8 (TG page 111). Explain that the page is the reproduction of an examination given to students in a public school in Brooklyn, New York. Brooklyn was home to many immigrants in 1897. Ask students how a course in "civil government" would help immigrant children adjust to life in the United States. (*It taught them citizenship and helped them understand American government.*)

3. CHECK UNDERSTANDING

Writing   Ask students to write a one-paragraph answer to question VII on Resource Page 8 (TG page 111): "Why should people who have no children be taxed to support the public schools?" Ask students to consider Mary Antin's feelings about education in their answers.

Thinking About the Chapter (Generalizing)   Mary's story is very personal and yet her book, *The Promised Land*, was popular because she touched on things common to all immigrants. In discussion identify some of Mary's experiences in America that reflect what any immigrant might have experienced.

JOHNS HOPKINS TEAM LEARNING

CHARTING THE COURSE OF *YICK WO* V. *HOPKINS*

1 EXTENDED CLASS PERIOD

FOCUS ACTIVITY

1. Share with students current newspaper accounts of two court cases, one civil and one criminal. Define the court-related vocabulary in the news articles and in Chapter 25 using the Definitions section of this page and by discussing the words and adding their meaning to a classroom vocabulary chart.

2. Review and discuss differences in the cases. For example: did the defendant break a law? Does the defendant face time in prison, a fine, or another penalty if convicted? To what higher court might the defendant appeal the outcome of the case? Ask interested students to track the cases in the news and report periodically on their status.

STUDENT LEARNING ACTIVITY/DRAWING CONCLUSIONS

1. Guide the students in reading Chapter 25 by having them pause at the appropriate places to
• define the court-related vocabulary.
• identify and discuss each step of the case.
• record information on a sheet entitled *Flowchart of the Case*.
Individual flowcharts should contain the following headings in order:

1. Arrest
2. Trial in Local Court
3. Appeal
4. Trial in California Supreme Court
5. Appeal
6. Trial in United States Supreme Court

2. **Circulate and Monitor**   Check students' work on the flowchart and understanding of court-related vocabulary.

3. Divide the class into teams and assign each team the questions below relating to *Yick Wo* v. *Hopkins*. Teams can use information in Chapter 25 and in other sources to prepare answers.
• Do police have the right to enforce the law arbitrarily?
• Do aliens have the same rights as citizens under the law?
• Do you agree or disagree with the Supreme Court ruling in the case of *Yick Wo* v. *Hopkins*? Support your viewpoint.

4. **Sharing Information**   Teams can use **Numbered Heads** to present their answers and viewpoints.

Definitions

Civil court—court that tries cases in which no criminal laws have been broken.

Criminal court—court that tries cases in which criminal laws have been broken.

Local court—first court (local/lower) to try civil or criminal cases.

State court—court that hears appeals from the local court; judge determines if justice has been served.

Supreme Court—highest court in the U.S. The nine justices hear appeals from local and state courts and interpret and uphold the rights and liberties guaranteed by the Constitution.

Appeal—to take a case to a higher court if not satisfied with the decision

Brief—written legal argument

Alien—person who is not a citizen

SUMMARIZING PART 5

Part 5 Check-Up   Use Check-Up 5 (TG page 101) to assess student learning in Part 5.

ALTERNATE ASSESSMENT

Ask students to write an essay answering one of the following questions, which link the big ideas across chapters:

1. Making Connections   How did increased immigration affect prejudice in the late 1800s? (*Students should cite examples such as the Know-Nothing Party and the Chinese Exclusion Act, as well as understanding the underlying tensions that fanned racist and nativist sentiments.*)

2. Making Connections   What was the link between passage of the 15th Amendment and the women's suffrage movement? (*The extension of the vote to black men made women more keenly aware of their own lack of rights as citizens.*)

USING THE RUBRICS

To assess these writing assignments, group projects, and activities, scoring rubrics have been provided at the back of this Teaching Guide. Be sure to explain the rubrics to your students.

DEBATING THE ISSUES

Use the topic below to stimulate debate.

Resolved   That Congress was wrong to pass the Chinese Exclusion Act of 1882. (Have some students speak against the Act, citing contributions by the Chinese. Refer these students to Chapter 13. Have others speak in favor of the Act as members of the Know-Nothings. Others might pose as "knowledgeable" economists who favor the Act out of concern about the economic depression.)

MAKING ETHICAL JUDGMENTS

The following question asks students to consider issues of ethics.

Suppose you lived in the late 1800s. How would you answer the following questions raised by the author on page 125: "What makes a citizen? Are women citizens?" Now skim Chapters 22-28. Which individuals would probably share your views? Have students support their choices with evidence from the text.

PROJECTS AND ACTIVITIES

Analyzing a Quote   Working in small groups, ask students to paraphrase the quote by Carl Schurz on page 112. (Encourage students to look up unfamiliar words in the dictionary.) Call on volunteers to read their revisions aloud. Then have them complete the following sentence: "I, Carl Schurz, believe America is the school for liberty because...."

Identifying Points of View   Read these lines from the poem by Emma Lazarus: *Give me your tired, your poor/Your huddled masses yearning to breathe free/The wretched refuse of your teeming shore/Send these, the homeless, tempest-tost, to me/I lift my lamp beside the golden door.* Then ask students how each of the following people might react to hearing these lines: a member of the Know-Nothing Party, Jacob Riis, Mary Antin.

Identifying Prejudice   Working in small groups, have students analyze the advertisement on page 121. Ask students to list techniques used by the ad designer to bias opinion against the Chinese. For example, what does the use of Uncle Sam show? (*that it's "patriotic" to kick out the Chinese*) Suppose such an ad ran today. How would people react to it? Why?

Conducting Mock Trials   Divide the class into two groups. Have one group prepare a mock trial reenacting *Yick Wo* v. *Hopkins*. Have the other group prepare a mock trial of Susan B. Anthony with Belva Lockwood defending Anthony. Instruct lawyers for the defense to state clearly the issues of justice involved in each case.

Using Historical Imagination   As the author requests on page 137, students should imagine that they are President Grant and have received Belva Lockwood's letter. Have them write letters in response.

Designing Historical Posters   Have students design posters for Women's History Month, which takes place in March. Working individually or in small groups, they can draw posters illustrating the legal and political "firsts" mentioned in Part 5.

Using Historical Imagination   Have students imagine they are Irish immigrants who have come to New York City, fleeing the Great Irish Famine of 1845–1850. Have them use the library/media center to research the famine. Then, have them write journal entries describing the famine, their flight to the US, and what kinds of conditions they found in New York City.

LOOKING AHEAD

Analyzing a Quote

In 1887, on the hundredth birthday of the Constitution, President Grover Cleveland declared:

> *Every American citizen should on this centennial day rejoice in their citizenship....He should rejoice because our Constitution...has survived so long, and also because...[the American people] have demonstrated so fully the strength and value of popular rule.*

Use this quote to launch a discussion of the meaning of citizenship in 1887. Who enjoyed its benefits? Who did not? Tell students that Part 6 takes a look at the United States as it entered the second century of its existence.

PART 6
TOWARD A NEW CENTURY

THE BIG IDEAS

To celebrate its one-hundredth birthday, the United States organized a grand Centennial Exposition. Explained one pamphlet:

During the past century the progress of the nation in invention and manufactures has been wonderful....To bring together all the evidences of this progress, and to combine in one location the engines of industry and their products...we are to have in the good city of Philadelphia an International Exhibition, to open May 10th, 1876.

The changes since 1776 had been staggering. Many problems still faced the nation. But the "evidences of progress" at the Centennial Exposition convinced many people that the nation might reach for perfection. Part 6 provides a glimpse of the nation at age 100.

INTRODUCING PART 6

SETTING GOALS
Introduce Part 6 by asking students to define *century* and *millennium* and to speculate why as a country we celebrate these milestones.

To set goals for Part 6, tell students that they will
• describe how the country had changed between 1776 and 1876.
• assess the problems of the country in 1876.
• evaluate Edison's inventions and his contributions to American life.

SETTING A CONTEXT FOR READING
Thinking About the Big Ideas   You might begin discussion of Part 6 by writing *change* on the chalkboard. Brainstorm with students to name as many major changes in the United States between 1776 and 1876 as they can. Distinguish positive and negative changes. If students had lived in 1876, which two changes might have given them the most pride?

Comparing and Contrasting   Tell students that in Chapters 29-31 author Joy Hakim makes many comparisons of the nation's achievements and problems after 100 years of existence. Ask students to note and discuss as many of these comparisons as they can.

SETTING A CONTEXT IN SPACE AND TIME
Using Maps   Have students use the blank U.S. political map in the back of their sutdy guides to outline and label the states that made up the United States in 1876.

Understanding Change Over Time Refer students to the time line on pages 156-157. Suppose the ghosts of the nation's founders revisited the nation on its 100th birthday. What changes might they find the most surprising? What changes would they find most welcome? Why?

READING NONFICTION

Analyzing Word Choice

Have partners find and list descriptive words or figurative language the author uses in her you-are-there account of the Centennial Exposition. Which words convey excitement? What synonyms, similes, or metaphors does the author use to give a vivid impression of the scene? Ask partners to then write a paragraph using some of the language they listed to write their own account of visiting the Centennial.

LINKING DISCIPLINES

History/Art

Ask students to look at the photographs and engravings in the chapter and explain why each one is symbolic of the nation's centennial.

ACTIVITIES/JOHNS HOPKINS TEAM LEARNING

See the Student Team Learning Activity on TG page 83.

CHAPTER 29 — 100 CANDLES

PAGES 146–150

1 Class Period   Homework: Student Study Guide p. 34

Chapter Summary

The Centennial Exposition in Philadelphia in 1876 celebrated American ingenuity and inventiveness. The marvels unveiled at the fair foreshadowed even greater achievements to come.

Key Vocabulary

centennial   exposition

1. CONNECT

Ask students why a mere 100 years of existence was considered such a milestone for the United States. (*The United States and its government was an experiment that many people expected to fail. The fact that the country had survived and prospered despite civil war and other problems, meant that those predictions of failure were wrong.*)

2. UNDERSTAND

1. Read the chapter. Discuss: What were some of the reasons that people were excited about the nation's 100th birthday? (*the success of the experiment in self-government, surviving a civil war, a thriving nation*) What was one of the purposes of the Women's Building? (*to show that women's inventiveness and artistry went beyond needle and thread*)
2. Explain that Susan B. Anthony and other representatives of women's suffrage groups were not allowed to speak at the Centennial Exposition's Fourth of July celebration as part of the official program. Instead they met outside the official event area and distributed the Declaration of the Rights of Women to a large crowd. Discuss whether the suffragists should have been included in the official celebration.

3. CHECK UNDERSTANDING

Writing   Ask students to write a postcard from the Centennial Exposition describing some of the exhibits and explaining which one was the writer's favorite.

Thinking About the Chapter (Analyzing) Discuss the author's question, "Besides inventions and material things, what had America achieved in its first hundred years?" (*Students should note ways in which liberty and justice had grown.*)

30 HOW WERE THINGS IN 1876?

PAGES 151–153

NOTE FROM THE AUTHOR

How do you teach about right and wrong? Through stories—the stories of heroes, heroines, and villains. You may get away with misbehavior in the long run, but hardly anyone escapes the judgment of history.

1 Class Period   Homework: Student Study Guide p. 34

Chapter Summary

The ideal of "equality for all" still lay beyond the reach of many Americans. But the fact that the Constitution had endured the test of civil war convinced most people that the United States would continue to change for the better.

Key Vocabulary

exports   stagnating
imports   middle class

1. CONNECT

Write *American* on the chalkboard and ask students to brainstorm a list of adjectives describing Americans in 1876. *(inventive, artistic, patriotic, forward-looking, immigrant)*

2. UNDERSTAND

1. Read the chapter. Discuss: In 1876, what were some of the things in which Americans could take pride? (*Constitution, end of slavery, growing population and trade, written guarantees of justice such as the 14th Amendment*) What were some of the problems facing the nation? (*injustices such as treatment of black Americans, lack of the vote for women, huge income gaps, treatment of Native Americans*)
2. Ask: What is meant by "two nations"? (*the rich and the poor*) Identify some of the examples of these two nations in this chapter. (*starvation in New York City where one of the richest men in the world lived; fancy parties and abandoned children; expensive parties and child labor*)

3. CHECK UNDERSTANDING

Writing   Ask students to take the role of reporters assigned to interview a boy garment worker (pictured on page 151) and William Vanderbilt (whose parties are described on page 153). As reporters, have students write a list of questions to ask each interviewee.

Thinking About the Chapter (Hypothesizing)   Pose this question to students: if time travel were possible, and you could go back to 1876, what would you take from our day to show people living then? Why?

READING NONFICTION

Analyzing Graphic Aids

Refer to the time line on pages 156-157. Ask students to identify the time span (*80 years*), the period (*10 years*), and the time period during which Edison made the inventions discussed in Chapter 31. (*1870-1880*) Have students discuss how this visual aid helps them understand how people lived and worked at different times during the 19th and early 20th centuries. (*Students can surmise what it was like to live without the light bulb, or how farmers' lives improved after 1830, or how the production of clothing changed after 1840.*)

GEOGRAPHY CONNECTIONS

Have students work in teams to analyze the database on U.S. Industry to the "U.S. Industry from Steamboats to Airplanes" map found at the back of *Reconstructing America*. Explain that each team must create questions to pose to the rest of the class. You may want to set up a contest in which teams vie to create the most questions regarding industry. Then focus their attention on questions of geographic distribution. Why, for example, would the invention and developments in the Midwest be concentrated around bodies of water? What can students extrapolate from the the preponderance of industry in the Northeast? Students should pose and answer each other's questions.

1 Class Period   **Homework: Student Study Guide p. 35**

Chapter Summary

The "invention factory" of Thomas Alva Edison set the pace of change as the nation entered its second century. Edison combined genius with hard work to give Americans phonographs, moving pictures, electricity, and more.

Key Vocabulary

Morse code	filament
telegraph	dynamos

1. CONNECT

Ask students to create a list of all the ways they have used electricity so far today, and how they expect to use it later. Talk about what they have done that would be impossible without electricity and list ways people did similar things without electricity.

2. UNDERSTAND

1. Read pages 154–155. Discuss: How did Edison turn disadvantages into advantages? (*Lack of schooling caused him to do things for himself; deafness allowed him to concentrate.*) Ask: What were some of the inventions to come out of Edison's "invention factory" in 1876? (*motion picture camera and projector, mimeograph, storage battery, locomotive, waxed paper*)
2. Read the rest of the chapter. Discuss the author's question: Would you lend money to a rumpled young man who said he could light a city? (*You might use this question to explore the risk side of free enterprise. What do investors have to gain or lose?*) Why does the author call Edison "a practical genius"? (*Many of his inventions, such as his improvement on the electric light bulb, were for everyone, not just the rich.*)

3. CHECK UNDERSTANDING

Writing   Ask students to write an ad for one of Edison's inventions. Suggest that they appeal to the readers' interest in progress.

Thinking About the Chapter (Analyzing Character)   Engage students in a discussion of Edison's character traits. Which ones helped to make him a successful, prolific inventor?

JOHNS HOPKINS TEAM LEARNING

TIME CAPSULE FOR 1876

FOCUS ACTIVITY

1. With students, create a class Top Ten list of the major accomplishments of our day. Then create a list of three or four Problems to Solve in the next 10 years. Encourage discussion of the choices, always asking why the accomplishment should be included.

2. Have students evaluate the accomplishments on the Top Ten list and vote on the single most important accomplishment of the United States in our time. Make sure students explain the reasons for their choice.

STUDENT TEAM LEARNING ACTIVITY/IDENTIFYING MAIN IDEAS

1. Divide the class into teams and present the following scenario: The year 1876 is drawing to a close and the Centennial Exposition is over. Before the exposition is dismantled, its organizers have asked your team to visit and decide which items and ideas should be placed in a time capsule. The team is to choose the Top Ten achievements and changes in the United States during its first 100 years. Be sure to consider inventions and material things, as well as the ways in which liberty has grown and justice has been secured.

2. Teams should visit the exposition by reading Chapters 29 and 30. After team members decide on their Top Ten choices for the time capsule, ask them to write a brief description of each selection.

3. Challenge each team to come up with a list of the three most important Problems to Solve in the next 100 years, from 1876 to 1976. This list will also go in the time capsule.

4. If necessary, provide some examples of accomplishments and problems to solve:
- the Statue of Liberty torch, representing the immigrants who came to, and are helping to build, America
- a sewing machine, symbolizing the change from hand-sewn to machine-sewn clothing
- the Fourteenth Amendment, which redefined citizenship
- feeding hungry children in the big cities

5. Circulate and Monitor Answer and ask questions to guide students in their work.

6. Sharing Information Use **Numbered Heads** for each team to share its time capsule contents. Ask teams to explain how they decided what to include in their time capsules.

SUMMARIZING PART 6

Part 6 Check-Up

Use Check-Up 6 (TG page 102) to assess student learning in Part 6.

LOOKING AHEAD

Analyzing a Quote

Not long after the Civil War ended, the governor of Indiana commented on the treatment of blacks in the North.

> *We not only exclude them from voting, we exclude them from testifying in courts of justice. We exclude them from our public schools, and we make it unlawful...for them to come into the state.*

Read this quote aloud, without identifying the geographic background of the speaker. Ask students whether they think the speaker was from the North or South. Use this activity to lead into a discussion of the widespread prejudice against blacks in the late 1800s.

ALTERNATE ASSESSMENT

Ask students to write an essay answering the following question, which links the big ideas across chapters:

Making Connections   What was the connection between the growth of technology in the late 1800s and the American belief in progress? (*Inventions proved that the nation was moving ahead. Many people believed other areas of life would improve too.*)

DEBATING THE ISSUES

Use the following topic to stimulate debate.

Resolved   That people should boycott the Centennial Exposition to protest the denial of rights to some Americans. (Some students can speak for black Americans, Native Americans, and women, all of whom still failed to enjoy equality. Others should defend the Centennial as a celebration of what the nation had accomplished.)

MAKING ETHICAL JUDGMENTS

The following question asks students to consider issues of ethics.

Suppose you are a very rich person in 1876. What, if any, responsibilities do you have toward the poor? (This is a tough question. Encourage students to debate the responsibilities that the privileged have toward the less privileged.)

USING THE RUBRICS

To assess these writing assignments, group projects, and activities, scoring rubrics have been provided at the back of this Teaching Guide. Be sure to explain the rubrics to your students.

PROJECTS AND ACTIVITIES

Analyzing a Quote   In 1833, the chief of the Patent Office resigned, saying: "Everything seems to have been done. I just don't see how anything else can be invented." Ask students why this official would have been surprised by the Centennial Exposition.

Illustrating an Idea   To show inequalities in American life in 1876, have students draw posters entitled *The Two Faces of America*. Posters might show freedoms enjoyed by some people and not by others, or they might focus on gaps between rich and poor.

Writing a News Story   Challenge students to imagine they are foreign reporters on the day Edison switched on the lights in New York City. Assign them to write a news story on this latest triumph of "American ingenuity."

THE BIG IDEAS

In 1897, a professor at Atlanta University named W. E. B. DuBois delivered a civil rights speech. Said DuBois:

> [A]n American, a Negro, two souls, two thoughts, two unreconciled strivings....The history of the American Negro is the history of this strife....He would not bleach the Negro soul in a flood of white Americanism....He simply wishes to make it possible for a man to be both a Negro and an American, without being cursed.

With African Americans bowing under the heavy hand of Jim Crow, DuBois called upon African Americans to claim their dual heritage. He demanded justice amid a time of segregation and lynchings. Not all African Americans agreed with DuBois. But his ideas planted seeds that would bear fruit at a later time. Part 7 describes the laws and practices that sought to crush the African American spirit and the people who worked to inspire black dignity amid this crisis.

PART 7 THE UNFINISHED JOURNEY

INTRODUCING PART 7

SETTING GOALS

Introduce Part 7 by looking back to Reconstruction. Ask students: Which group of Americans was excluded from the general mood of celebration in 1876? Is it a coincidence that the end of Reconstruction and the abandonment of the defense of black Southerners' rights came at a time of great national prosperity?

To set goals for Part 7, tell students that they will
• learn about the segregation in the South under Jim Crow.
• examine the character and career of Ida B. Wells and her campaign against lynching (mob rule).
• compare the philosophies and achievements of two very different black Americans of the late 19th century.

SETTING A CONTEXT FOR READING

Thinking About the Big Ideas   You might open discussion by writing the title of Part 7 on the chalkboard: "The Unfinished Journey." Have students skim the chapters of the Part. With whose journey is Part 7 mainly concerned? (*African Americans*) If the journey of African Americans was unfinished, what can students infer about the journey of the entire nation? (*It too was unfinished.*) Use this discussion to lead students to understand that the nation's strivings would not end until all its peoples enjoyed justice.

Making Judgments   Explain to students that in Chapters 32-37, Joy Hakim encourages readers to make judgments against the terrorist tactics used in many parts of the country to discourage black people from exercising their rights. She also encourages readers to judge favorably people like Ida B. Wells, Booker T. Washington, and W. E. B. DuBois.

SETTING A CONTEXT IN SPACE AND TIME

Interpreting Historical Maps   Tell students that between 1882 and 1958, mob murders, or executions without benefit of trial, were reported in every state except Rhode Island, Connecticut, New Hampshire, and Massachusetts. The following statistics concern those states in which more than 50 percent of the mob murders were committed against African Americans.

NUMBER	STATES
1-9	NY, PA, NJ, DE
10-49	WV, MD, OH, IL
50-199	MO, VA, NC, SC
200-399	FL, AL, TN, KY, AR, LA
400 or more	TX, MS, GA

Source: Historical Atlas of the United States (National Geographic)

Distribute copies of the U.S. political map found in the resource pages section of this guide or have students use the map in their study guides to show this data geographically. Have them make a legend that shows the data by color, and color in and label the states mentioned. Then, discuss the following questions: In which region were African Americans at the greatest risk of violence? (*the South*) Were African Americans safe in the North? (*no*)

Understanding Change Over Time   Refer students to the Chronology on page 184. Tell them to examine the dates for the years after the end of Reconstruction (1876). How might black Americans have described these years? (*as years in which they suffered injustices*) Encourage students to name specific events that support their inferences.

1 Class Period   Homework: Student Study Guide p. 36

Chapter Summary

Hopes of equality from Reconstruction were dashed by the decision in *Plessy* v. *Ferguson*. The only victor in the case was a vaudeville-inspired fool named Jim Crow.

Key Vocabulary

segregation	franchise	poll tax
Jim Crow	white supremacy	lynching

1. CONNECT

Write *Yick Wo* v. *Hopkins* and *Plessy* v. *Ferguson* on the chalkboard. Ask students to recall the issue and the outcome in *Yick Wo*. Tell students that in *Plessy* v. *Ferguson* the Court ruled on the constitutionality of racial segregation.

2. UNDERSTAND

1. Read pages 160–163, through the first paragraph. Discuss: What were race relations like in the North and South before the Civil War? (*North: no slavery, segregation; South: slavery, no segregation*) Discuss: By the end of Reconstruction, how had these relations changed? (*North: segregation by habit continued; South: legal segregation enforced by violence began.*) What does "equal protection of the law" mean? (*that laws apply equally to all people*) Were the Jim Crow laws constitutional or unconstitutional? What about laws and taxes that prevented blacks from voting? (*Help students use provisions from the 14th and 15th Amendments in their decisions.*)
2. Read the rest of the chapter. Discuss: What was the issue in *Plessy* v. *Ferguson*? (*Were "separate but equal" laws constitutional?*) What did the Supreme Court rule? (*It upheld these laws, opening the way for legal segregation.*)

3. CHECK UNDERSTANDING

Writing   Ask students to write a paragraph explaining what Frederick Douglass meant when he said, "There is no Negro problem." (See the box on page 164.)

Thinking About the Chapter (Hypothesizing)   Engage students in speculating what would have been the result in the South and in the North if the Court had ruled in *Plessy* v. *Ferguson* that segregation was unconstitutional.

ACTIVITIES/JOHNS HOPKINS TEAM LEARNING

See the Student Team Learning Activity on TG page 92.

HISTORY ARCHIVES

A History of US Sourcebook
#68, From John Marshall Harlan, dissenting opinion in *Plessy v. Ferguson* (1896)

READING NONFICTION

Analyzing Rhetorical Devices
In the second paragraph, have students find the author's opinion of the Jim Crow laws. (*an "evil policy"*) Then ask them to find examples of how the author personifies Jim Crow laws. (*"Jim Crow began dancing across the Southern land." "Jim Crow was going wild."*) Discuss with students the effect of these personifications. (Students may be confused by the positive connotations of "dancing" or "going wild.")

MEETING INDIVIDUAL NEEDS

Some students may be confused by the term "Jim Crow." They should understand the difference between Jim Crow, the racist caricature performed by a white actor and popular with white audiences in the 19th century (shown in the pictures on pages 160 and 163) and Jim Crow, a system of racial segregation. For black Americans, "living under Jim Crow" meant being restricted in where you could go, what you could do, and whom you could associate with. The penalty for breaking the Jim Crow laws and customs could be death.

Have students use a map of the United States to locate the following places important in Ida B. Wells's life: Holly Springs, Mississippi; Memphis, Tennessee; New York, New York; Chicago, Illinois.

CHAPTER 33 | IDA B. WELLS

PAGES 165–169

CHAPTER 34 | LYNCHING MEANS KILLING BY A MOB

PAGES 170–173

1 Class Period   **Homework: Student Study Guide p. 37**

Chapter Summaries

Ida B. Wells shouldered responsibility at an early age—not only for her family, but for the African American struggle for equality. She risked her life by refusing to abandon the struggle for justice. After slavery, one of the darkest blots on our history was the era in which vigilante justice killed thousands of innocent people. To effect change, Wells spread the word about crimes against black people and championed anti-lynching laws.

Key Vocabulary

vigilante justice   anarchy

1. CONNECT

Write *mob* and *vigilante* on the chalkboard and discuss what they meant in the South after the Civil War.

2. UNDERSTAND

1. Read Chapter 33. Discuss: What character traits describe Ida B. Wells as a teenager? (*courageous, honest, responsible*) How did Wells respond to segregation when she moved to Memphis? (*She fought it, physically and in a court of law.*)
2. Read Chapter 34. Ask: How does vigilante justice violate the 14th Amendment? (*deprives victims of due process of law and the right to a fair trial*) Discuss: What actions did Ida B. Wells take to protest lynchings? (*collected and publicized statistics on lynching, wrote about them, organized boycotts to demonstrate the economic power of black Americans*) What price did Wells pay for her courage? (*She had to leave the South for 30 years to avoid physical harm.*)
3. Distribute Resource Page 9 (TG page 112) and discuss the contents. Have students answer the questions and evaluate the effectiveness of this call to action.

3. CHECK UNDERSTANDING

Writing   Ask students to write a one-page biography of Ida B. Wells explaining her life and work to young readers.

Thinking About the Chapter (Evaluating)   Discuss this question with students: What was Ida B. Wells's greatest contribution? Why should she be remembered today?

35 | A MAN AND HIS TIMES
PAGES 174-176

1 Class Period   **Homework: Student Study Guide p. 38**

Chapter Summary
Booker T. Washington placed economic freedom ahead of other types of freedom. His judgment grew out of the times in which he lived—a time in which many African Americans in the South barely scratched a living from the land.

Key Vocabulary
vocational   soil-exhausting crops

1. CONNECT

Read aloud the quote from Booker T. Washington's *Autobiography* which opens Chapter 35. Tell students that the author became one of the best-known men in the United States by the end of the 19th century.

2. UNDERSTAND

1. Read Chapter 35. Discuss: What obstacle did Booker T. Washington overcome to gain an education? (*poverty*) What example did he set for other people? (*the value of hard work*) Discuss answers to the author's question on page 175, "Do you think that statement was wise or foolish?" (*Wise: Washington's position was practical, given the extreme prejudice at the time; Foolish: Change would never come unless African Americans took uncompromising stands.*)
2. Discuss: What advice did Booker T. Washington offer black students at Tuskegee? (*win economic freedom before battling for other freedoms*) How did he intend to win economic freedom? (*through technical training*)

3. CHECK UNDERSTANDING

Writing   Ask students to take the role of a fund raiser and write a letter to potential contributors describing Tuskegee Institute under Booker T. Washington and the importance of having a scientist such as George Washington Carver at Tuskegee.

Thinking About the Chapter (Synthesizing)   Have students reread the quotes in the chapter from Washington's *Autobiography*. Compare Washington's description of getting an education as "getting into paradise" to Mary Antin's attitude toward education (Chapter 28). Discuss the similarities in the lives of these two very different Americans that made education so important to them.

HISTORY ARCHIVES
A History of US Sourcebook
#67, From Booker T. Washington, *Address at the Atlanta Exposition* (1895)

READING NONFICTION
Analyzing Primary and Secondary Sources
Point out the author's comment on page 176 that Booker T. Washington "spoke so well that he often left audiences cheering." Ask students how the author knows this. (*She must have read primary sources that verified this fact.*) Then have volunteers read aloud some of the quotes from Washington's autobiography. Ask students how reading from this primary source helps them understand the author's comment, and discuss how Washington's ability as a writer probably contributed to his being a mesmerizing speaker.

Invite a volunteer to read aloud the poem by Dudley Randall on page 180. Ask students to discuss which leader's ideas the poet admires more, "Booker T." or "W. E. B.," or if students think the poet's purpose is only to focus readers on two different but valid ideas.

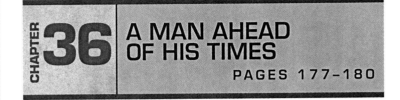

CHAPTER **36** A MAN AHEAD OF HIS TIMES

PAGES 177–180

1 Class Period   Homework: Student Study Guide p. 39

Chapter Summary

W. E. B. DuBois rejected Booker T. Washington's approach to change. In words similar to those of the civil rights movement of the 1950s, DuBois demanded nothing less than full equality.

Key Vocabulary

color line   anti-Semitism   civil-rights movement

1. CONNECT

Write the chapter title on the chalkboard and discuss the connotations of the phrase. Ask: Where is a person more likely to be comfortable—"of his times" or "ahead of his times"? Ask them to speculate about the effects "a man ahead of his times" might have on other people.

2. UNDERSTAND

1. Read pages 177–179, through "father of the civil rights movement of the twentieth century." Discuss: How did Washington and DuBois differ in their approaches to relations with white Americans? (*Washington: compromised, traded off social equality for economic opportunity; DuBois: refused to compromise with anyone on equality*)
2. Read the rest of the chapter. Discuss: How did Dubois's childhood experiences differ from Washington's? (*DuBois: free; experienced democracy of New England town meetings; taught pride in his African heritage; received a prestigious Harvard education; Washington: first a slave and then poor; worked very hard to pay for education*) What did DuBois mean by "Responsibility is the first step in responsibility"? (*People learn responsibility only by being given the opportunity to be responsible.*)

3. CHECK UNDERSTANDING

Writing   Read aloud the poem on page 180. Discuss the contrast between W. E. B. and Booker T. Work together to create a new verse where Ida B. Wells's ideas are incorporated into the poem. The refrain for that verse might be: "As for me, said Ida B., with W. E. B. I must agree."

Thinking About the Chapter (Analyzing)   Discuss DuBois's idea about the "double inheritance" of each American. Ask volunteers to describe their own double inheritance and explain how diversity, in the author's words, "makes America special."

1 Class Period   Homework: Student Study Guide p. 40

Chapter Summary

Although America was far from perfect at the end of the 19th century, it was headed in the direction of freedom and equality for all of its citizens.

Key Vocabulary

city on a hill   class distinction

1. CONNECT

Write on the chalkboard the names of some of the people introduced in Book 7: Lee Yick, Carl Schurz, Ida B. Wells, Chief Joseph, W. E. B. DuBois, Susan B. Anthony, Mary Antin. Then write: "All men are created equal." Ask students: Do you agree with Joy Hakim that "the world has not been the same since those words were written"? What did those words mean to the people listed on the chalkboard?

2. UNDERSTAND

1. Read the chapter. Discuss: What tools did the nation's founders give us for perfecting the nation? (*the ideals in the Declaration of Independence and the Constitution*)
2. Discuss: What were some of the "layers of democracy" that later generations added to the promise of freedom? (*You might give students the option of answering this question in written form or of presenting the answer in the form of an "idea pyramid." The promises of the Declaration can form the base, with other advances forming new levels reaching for the pinnacle, or perfection.*)

3. CHECK UNDERSTANDING

Writing   Ask students to write a one-paragraph answer to the caption question under the photograph of the Tucker brothers on page 181. Have students include the changes that would be needed before the Tuckers could enjoy life, liberty, and the pursuit of happiness.

Thinking About the Chapter (Evaluating)   Ask students if they agree with these statements by the author, and why: "Government for the people isn't easy because those with the loudest voices drown out the weak and powerless" (page 182). "America wasn't perfect but it certainly was heading in the direction of freedom, equality, and happiness for all its citizens" (page 183).

READING NONFICTION

Analyzing Graphic Aids

Have students look at the pictures that illustrate Chapter 37. As a glimpse of Americans in the late 19th century, who is missing? (*Native Americans, Asians*) Of the five chapter illustrations, which immigrant group is represented twice? (*Germans*) Have students choose illustrations from other chapters in the book that they would suggest including in Chapter 37 to make it more representative.

JOHNS HOPKINS TEAM LEARNING

CHALLENGING JIM CROW

1 CLASS PERIOD

FOCUS ACTIVITY

1. Have students count off in order to divide the class into two teams, "odds" and "evens." Give the following directions: It is your responsibility to make rules that will separate you from the other team (the "others") as you travel to and from school. The "others" are inferior to you and so must be kept apart. Ask the teams to consider whether their rules will require the "others" to travel in a different section of the same school bus, on different buses, or on no bus. Ask: Will you allow the "others" to drive? To drive on school grounds? To walk on the same sidewalks?

2. After about 10 minutes, use **Numbered Heads** to have teams share their rules. Ask: How would you feel if you were empowered to make rules like this? If you were subjected to rules like this?

STUDENT TEAM LEARNING ACTIVITY/UNDERSTANDING *PLESSY V. FERGUSON*

1. Divide the class into several small teams and ask them to read pages 163-164 and make a list of the following:
- the facts in *Plessy* v. *Ferguson*
- the issue in *Plessy* v. *Ferguson*
- the opinion of the Supreme Court in *Plessy* v. *Ferguson*

2. Circulate and Monitor Visit each team as students finish reading the chapter and identify the facts, issue, and opinion in the case.

3. Invite teams to write and act out a scene based on the circumstances that precipitated *Plessy* v. *Ferguson* in 1896. Assign each team one of the following scenes:
- Homer Plessy's friends urge him to test the Louisiana law that requires separation of rail passengers by race and Plessy agrees.
- Plessy gets on the train and sits in the white section of the railroad car. The conductor approaches Plessy and is informed that he is black. Plessy refuses to change seats.
- The police arrest Plessy and remove him from the train and take him to jail.

4. Sharing Information Have teams present their scenes in chronological order, creating a skit based on the incident that launched *Plessy* v. *Ferguson.*

5. Lead the class in a discussion of how segregation harms both races, but especially the minority race. Use questions such as the following to spark discussion:
- What conditions in the United States made it possible for the Supreme Court to uphold segregationist policy in its decision in *Plessy* v. *Ferguson*?
- In what way did the Court's racist interpretation of the Fourteenth and Fifteenth Amendments violate the original intent of those amendments?

ASSESSMENT

Part 7 Check-Up Use Check-Up 7 (TG page 103) to assess student learning in Part 7.

ALTERNATE ASSESSMENT
Ask students to write an essay answering one of the following questions, which link the big ideas across chapters:

1. Making Connections Who do you think Ida B. Wells would be most likely to support—Booker T. Washington or W. E. B. DuBois? Why? (*probably DuBois, because of his activist approach to change*)

2. Making Connections What was the connection between *Plessy* v. *Ferguson* and the spread of injustice against African Americans? (*The Supreme Court's ruling in the case institutionalized segregation in the United States and redefined the 14th Amendment.*)

DEBATING THE ISSUES
Use the topic below to stimulate debate.

Resolved That Booker T. Washington was right in compromising with whites until black Americans gained more economic clout. (The debate should include the voices of Washington, Wells, DuBois, and Montgomery. To heat up the debate even more, you might appoint a few white spokespersons such as Andrew Carnegie.)

MAKING ETHICAL JUDGMENTS
The following questions ask students to consider issues of ethics.

1. Put yourself in the shoes of Isaiah Montgomery. Given the backlash against blacks in Mississippi, would you have opposed the "Understanding Law"? (*Answers will vary, but have students weigh the force of hatred that blacks faced at the time.*)

2. The author asks whether there are times when people should take the law into their own hands. Have students state and explain their opinions. (*First discuss vigilante justice. Then look at alternatives, such as the citizen's arrest, the good Samaritan, the use of 911.*)

3. On page 180, the author asks, "What happens to you when you hate somebody?" (*After students express their feelings about hatred, discuss the difficulty of not hating when faced by prejudice. Ask students to analyze the effect on themselves when they feel hatred for someone or something.*)

PROJECTS AND ACTIVITIES
Showing Reasoned Judgment Frederick Douglass urged black Southerners not to flee the Jim Crow South. "[G]oing into

NOTE FROM THE AUTHOR
History is a natural with children. It is—or should be—all about people and ideas and adventures. That we have made it dull is the wonder.

USING THE RUBRICS
To assess these writing assignments, group projects, and activities, scoring rubrics have been provided at the back of this Teaching Guide. Be sure to explain the rubrics to your students.

LOOKING AHEAD

Making Predictions

End this book with a discussion of challenges the nation faced as it headed into the modern era. To kick off discussion, read this quote from Teddy Roosevelt's 1905 inaugural address:

Such growth in wealth, in population, and in power as this nation has seen...is inevitably accompanied by a like growth in the problems which are ever before a nation that rises to greatness.

Ask students what new issues the nation might have to tackle as it becomes an urban industrial nation. What issues might arise as it becomes a world power?

a strange land," he said, "is a confession...[that] equal rights and equal protection in any State...may be struck down by violence." Tell students to imagine they are black Southerners in 1880. Working in small groups, students should decide whether they will heed Douglass's advice or escape the repression.

Designing a Flowchart   To illustrate the process of judicial review, students can design a flowchart showing the way in which *Plessy* v. *Ferguson* reached the Supreme Court.

Using Primary Sources   Ask students to write a brief biography of Ida B. Wells that might appear in a book called *Crusaders for Justice*. Have them base their work on the quotations in Chapters 33 and 34.

Designing Posters   A slogan in the Memphis streetcar boycott organized by Wells read: "Do not trample on our pride by being 'jim crowed.' Walk!" Request volunteers to design posters illustrating this slogan.

Digging Deeper   The author wanted to include a chapter on George Washington Carver in the book—but there wasn't room. Have interested students write this chapter for her. Distribute copies to the class.

Use the following questions to help students pull together some of the major concepts and themes covered in this book. Note: You may wish to assign these as essay questions for assessment.

1. What changes did Radical Republicans try to bring to the South? Which, if any, of these changes succeeded? (*Students should focus on efforts to reshape southern society from the bottom up. First and foremost, the Radicals wanted to give power to black Southerners and take it from former Confederates. Although Reconstruction largely failed, the 14th and 15th Amendments gave future generations the tools to bring about more long-lasting changes.*)

2. In 1906, Senator Benjamin Tillman of South Carolina stood to address the Senate. The subject was the end of Reconstruction. Said Tillman: "It was in 1876, thirty years ago....Life ceased to be worth having on the terms under which we were living....[I]n desperation, we determined to take the government away from blacks." What techniques did white Southerners such as Tillman use "to take the government away from blacks"? (*Techniques include vigilante justice, voter fraud, use of poll taxes and literacy tests, and so on.*) Suppose you were a black senator from the South. How would you describe the same period in history? (*A black Senator might also say life "ceased to be worth having." However, the reasons would center on the injustices of raw terror and Jim Crow.*)

3. In 1870, a Dakota newspaper boasted: "Without the railroad it would have required a century to accomplish what has been done in five years." How would each of the following describe the changes brought by the railroad: (a) a Native American, (b) a cattle herder, (c) a homesteader? (*Answers will vary. But for Native Americans, the railroad meant destruction of the buffalo, a flood of settlers, and the end of a way of life. For a cattle herder, the railroad also ended a way of life as trains eliminated the long drives. For homesteaders, the railroads offered a route west and, in many cases, cheap land.*)

4. Mark Twain once said: "Nothing so much needs reforming as other people's habits." If you lived during the Gilded Age, which people's habits would you have most wanted to reform? Why? (*Answers will vary. Choices might include corrupt politicians such as Boss Tweed, lavish spenders such as William Vanderbilt, people opposed to women's suffrage, white supremacists.*)

5. What factors helped push immigrants out of Europe and Asia? What factors pulled them toward the United States? (*Push: war, lack of religious freedom, poverty, famine, etc. Pull: stable government, religious freedom, economic opportunity, ideals such as liberty and equality.*)

6. Imagine you are a student in 1876. Your teacher has just told you about a writing contest in celebration of the Centennial. The object is to write an essay or poem honoring the growth of

I like to ask children to write their own tests. They have to think to do that. Then I have them answer their own questions and someone else's as well.

American justice. The prize is a free trip to the Centennial Exposition. What information will you include in your essay or poem? *(Answers will vary, but students might touch on some of the points mentioned in Chapter 37.)*

7. Compare the ideas of Ida B. Wells, Booker T. Washington, and W. E. B. DuBois. What goal did all three of these African American leaders share? How did they differ in their methods of achieving this goal? *(All three worked to win better lives for African Americans. To win economic advancement, Washington was willing to compromise until whites learned to give up their prejudice. Neither Wells nor DuBois accepted compromise when it came to issues of civil rights.)*

CHECK-UP 1

Answering the following questions will help you understand and remember what you have read in Chapters 1-7. Write your answers on a separate sheet of paper.

1. Each person listed below played a part in shaping the direction of Reconstruction. Tell how each person took part in Reconstruction.
   a. Abraham Lincoln
   b. Andrew Johnson
   c. Mary Peake
   d. Charlotte Forten
   e. Blanche Bruce
   f. Hiram Revels
   g. Thaddeus Stevens
   h. Edmund G. Ross

2. The Civil War took place mostly in the South. So did Reconstruction. Imagine you are a federal agent visiting each of the following places at the times mentioned. Write down any problems that you might observe. Also note any activities that promote rebuilding of the region.
   a. Charleston, 1865
   b. Memphis and New Orleans, 1865-1866
   c. Port Royal, South Carolina, 1865-1866
   d. Atlanta, 1867-1870

3. Define each of the following terms. Then explain its significance to events of the time.
   a. Freedmen's Bureau
   b. martial law
   c. Military Reconstruction
   d. carpetbaggers
   e. scalawags
   f. impeachment

4. In 1870, the U.S. Census Bureau would find a larger nation—both in terms of physical size and population. How were people and land added to the United States during the 1860s?

5. During Reconstruction, an African American said: "It seemed like it took a long time for freedom to come. Everything just kept on like it was." How did each of the following work against change in the South?
   a. Ku Klux Klan
   b. black codes
   c. race riots

6. List the provisions of the Reconstruction Act. How do you think each of the following people would have responded to the provisions of the Act? Explain your answers.
   a. carpetbagger
   b. scalawag
   c. freedman or freedwoman
   d. former Confederate officer

7. Suppose you had been Thaddeus Stevens. What arguments would you have used to convince members of Congress to support impeachment proceedings?

8. Do you think that Johnson had a fair trial in the Senate? What evidence in the text supports your opinion?

9. Imagine you are the editor of an African American newspaper. Write an obituary on the death of Thaddeus Stevens.

10. **Thinking About the Big Ideas**   How did the 14th Amendment extend justice in the United States? How did it change the structure of United States government? How did it provide a tool for bringing about change in the decades ahead?

CHECK-UP 2

Answering the following questions will help you understand and remember what you have read in Chapters 8-10. Write your answers on a separate sheet of paper.

1. Suppose you are an author writing an historical narrative entitled "The Final Days of Reconstruction." Identify each of the following people. Then tell why each is important to your story.
   a. Robert Brown Elliot
   b. Jonathan C. Gibbs
   c. Mary Virginia Montgomery
   d. Jefferson Davis
   e. Ulysses S. Grant
   f. Wade Hampton
   g. Rutherford B. Hayes

2. You must also pick geographic settings for your book. What events related to Reconstruction took place at each of the following sites?
   a. Charleston, South Carolina
   b. Fort Monroe, Virginia
   c. Davis Bend
   d. Mound Bayou

3. Define each of these terms. Then explain how the term relates to the final years of Reconstruction.
   a. sharecropping
   b. poll tax
   c. lynching
   d. segregation
   e. redeemers

4. Some people describe the South Carolina constitutional convention as the start of "America's Second Revolution." What was so revolutionary about this meeting?

5. Write an advertisement that Benjamin Montgomery might have written to attract laborers to Davis Bend.

6. Suppose the Montgomery family hired you to defend their property rights at Davis Bend. What arguments would you use to challenge claims by Jefferson Davis? What does Davis's victory tell you about the rights of black Southerners in the late 1870s?

7. How did Ulysses S. Grant earn the nickname "Useless S. Grant"?

8. How did the provisions of the 13th, 14th, and 15th Amendments allow later reformers to challenge the following practices?
   a. poll taxes
   b. segregated railroad cars
   c. lynchings

9. **Thinking About the Big Ideas**   The author says that in the second half of the twentieth century a black minister would heal the old wounds and begin real Reconstruction in America. Who was that minister? (If you need a clue, look at the national holidays celebrated in the month of January.)

10. **Thinking About the Big Ideas**   How did Reconstruction legislatures attempt to increase justice in the South? Which of the changes sought by these governments are part of our life today?

CHECK-UP 3

Answering the following questions will help you understand and remember what you have read in Chapters 11-18. Write your answers on a separate sheet of paper.

1. Each person listed below played a part in this period of our history. Tell who each person was and what he or she did of importance.
   a. John Wesley Powell
   b. Elijah G. McCoy
   c. Joseph G. McCoy
   d. Jesse Chisholm
   e. Nat Love
   f. Elizabeth E. Johnson
   g. Leland Stanford
   h. George Pullman
   i. Willa Cather
   j. Cyrus McCormick
   k. George Washington Carver
   l. Crazy Horse
   m. Chief Joseph

2. What happened at each of these places? How were these events connected with the loss of Native American lands and cultures?
   a. Oklahoma Territory
   b. Promontory Point, Utah
   c. Little Big Horn River
   d. Pine Ridge Agency School, Dakota Territory
   e. Wounded Knee

3. Define each of these terms. Then explain its significance to the events of the time.
   a. capital
   b. Texas longhorns
   c. ties
   d. subsidy
   e. emigrant cars
   f. Homestead Act
   g. barbed wire
   h. prairie
   i. Morrill Act
   j. reservations

4. Suppose you were a member of one of the Plains peoples such as the Cheyenne or Sioux. How would you describe the Great Plains? Now suppose you were a homesteader. How would you describe the same land?

5. Write diary entries describing a typical cattle drive up the Chisholm Trail. Include descriptions of both the hardships and rewards of working the open range.

6. When the Union Pacific and the Central Pacific met, reporters from all over the country sent telegraph messages into their home offices. Write a twenty-five-word message that you might have sent on this historic occasion.

7. Write an advertisement that Joseph Glidden might have designed to convince homesteaders to buy his new product, barbed wire.

8. How did the wide-open geography of the Plains encourage the rise of commercial farming?

9. **Thinking About the Big Ideas**   Recall the speech by Chief Joseph after the United States government confined the Nez Perce to a land-poor reservation. How would Chief Joseph define the term *justice*?

10. **Thinking About the Big Ideas**   How did settlement of the Plains bring changes to Native Americans and to the nation as a whole?

CHECK-UP 4

Answering the following questions will help you understand and remember what you have read in Chapters 19-21. Write your answers on a separate sheet of paper.

1. Each person listed below played a key role in the events described in these chapters. Identify each person. Then tell whether each was a "schemer," a "dreamer," or both, and explain your answer.
   a. William Marcy Tweed
   b. Alfred Ely Beach
   c. George Washington Plunkitt
   d. Thomas Nast
   e. Phineas T. Barnum
   f. Mark Twain

2. The United States was a very diverse place by the late 1800s. Name the region in which each of the following places was located, and tell what the place was like at the time.
   a. New York City
   b. Hannibal, Missouri
   c. San Francisco, California
   d. Crede, Colorado

3. Define each of these terms. Then explain its significance to the events of the time.
   a. graft
   b. Tammany Hall
   c. political machines
   d. constituents
   e. fraud
   f. humbug
   g. robber barons
   h. reformers
   i. Gilded Age

4. When he was accused of corruption, Boss Tweed remarked: "As long as I count the votes, what are you going to do about it?"
   a. What insight does this give you into injustices at the time?
   b. How did reformers call Tweed's bluff?

5. According to George Washington Plunkitt, what was the difference between "dishonest graft" and "honest graft"? Why is all graft a threat to democratic government?

6. Imagine you are P. T. Barnum. You have decided to act as ring master on the opening night of your all-new three-ring circus. Write a brief speech announcing the lineup of events. (Keep in mind Barnum's own advice: "I saw everything depended on getting people to think, and talk, and become curious and excited over and about the, 'rare spectacle.'")

7. The author says that Mark Twain made Americans think about who we are and what we want to be. How do you think his books do that?

8. The author says that even in old age Mark Twain "could still think like a child, which isn't a bad thing." What do you think she means?

9. Thinking About the Big Ideas   The framers of the Constitution failed to foresee two political changes— the development of political parties and the rise of political machines. Which posed the greater threat to justice? Explain.

CHECK-UP 5

Answering the following questions will help you understand and remember what you have read in Chapters 22-28. Write your answers on a separate sheet of paper.

1. The people listed below each had ideas on liberty and justice in the United States. Identify each person. Then tell how each one viewed these ideals.
   a. Carl Schurz
   b. Jacob Riis
   c. Sheriff Hopkins
   d. Lee Yick (Yick Wo)
   e. Esther Morris
   f. Mildred Rutherford
   g. Susan B. Anthony
   h. Horace Greeley
   i. Belva Ann Lockwood

2. Each of the following places is related in some way to the growth of diversity in the United States. Tell what each place was and explain its link to diversity.
   a. Ellis Island
   b. Pulaski, Tennessee
   c. San Francisco
   d. Wyoming
   e. Rochester, New York

3. Define each of these terms. Then explain its significance to the events of the time.
   a. tenements
   b. steerage
   c. Golden Mountain
   d. nativism
   e. Chinese Exclusion Act
   f. aliens

4. Suppose you are a worker for the U.S. Census Bureau in 1890. Your job is to summarize the major changes in immigration in the past decade. What changes will you cite?

5. Near the end of the century, a Polish immigrant decided to return to Europe. Explained the woman: "We are going back to the Old Country. America *ne dobre* [not good]....The air *ne dobre*, the food *ne dobre*, the houses *ne dobre*." What living conditions faced by many immigrants might help explain her words?

6. Suppose you are Lee Yick. What arguments will you use to convince other Chinese laundry owners to join you in an appeal of your conviction for operating a laundry in a wooden building?

7. How were the 14th and 15th Amendments linked to the trials of Lee Yick and Susan B. Anthony?

8. Imagine you are a reporter for an eastern paper such as the *New York Times*. Write a brief news article on the Wyoming Tea Party.

9. Put yourself in Mary Antin's shoes on her first day at Boston's Latin School. Write a monologue that captures your private thoughts as you start elementary school in the United States.

10. **Thinking About the Big Ideas**   List some of the ideals that attracted immigrants to the United States. Then explain how these ideals helped unite the diverse peoples who came to this nation in the late 1800s.

CHECK-UP 6

Answering the following questions will help you understand and remember what you have read in Chapters 29-31. Write your answers on a separate sheet of paper.

1. Each person named below contributed to the pride that many Americans felt in the United States as it turned 100 years old. Tell who each person was, and explain how he or she contributed to American pride.
   - a. Mrs. E. D. Gillespie
   - b. George Henry Corliss
   - c. Alexander Graham Bell
   - d. Elizabeth Cady Stanton
   - e. Walter Camp
   - f. Thomas Alva Edison
   - g. Grosvenor Porter Lowrey

2. Imagine that you are writing an article called "Signs of Progress" about the United States at the end of the 1800s. Why would you describe each of these places in your article?
   - a. Philadelphia
   - b. Menlo Park
   - c. New York City

3. Define each of these terms. Then explain its significance to the events of the times.
   - a. centennial
   - b. exposition
   - c. consent of the governed
   - d. exports
   - e. middle class
   - f. filament

4. Put yourself in the shoes of President Grant. You must write a brief speech for the opening ceremonies at the Centennial Exposition. What will you say about the state of the nation in 1876?

5. If you could visit the Centennial, which attraction would you most want to see? Why?

6. Some people in the 19th century described the rich and the poor as "two nations." What do you think they meant by this remark?

7. The first news of the battle of Little Bighorn reached eastern newspapers on July 5, 1876. This was in the middle of the Centennial Exposition. Create a mock dialogue between two fairgoers who have just learned about the defeat of George Armstrong Custer.

8. Thomas Alva Edison recruited some of the nation's most talented inventors to work at Menlo Park. Write a help-wanted ad that Edison might have written for a new assistant.

9. Thomas Edison said: "Genius is ninety-nine percent perspiration and one percent inspiration." What do you think he meant? Do you agree? Why or why not?

10. **Thinking About the Big Ideas** A magazine reporter who visited Philadelphia in 1876 wrote: "The thousands who move among the Centennial marvels…wonder how their poor forefathers [and foremothers] lived a hundred years ago." What changes had taken place to make Americans think about this question?

CHECK-UP 7

Answering the following questions will help you understand and remember what you have read in Chapters 32-37. Write your answers on a separate sheet of paper.

1. Each person below played a key role in the lives of African Americans in the closing years of the 19th century. Tell who each person was, and explain how he or she took a stand on civil rights.
   a. Homer Plessy
   b. John M. Harlan
   c. Ida B. Wells
   d. Booker T. Washington
   e. W. E. B. DuBois

2. Suppose you are putting together a guidebook entitled *African American Historical Landmarks in the United States*. Why might you include each of these places in your book?
   a. Holly Springs, Mississippi
   b. Hampton, Virginia
   c. Tuskegee, Alabama
   d. Great Barrington, Massachusetts
   e. Niagara Falls

3. Define each of the following terms. Then tell how each pair is linked.
   a. segregation, Jim Crow
   b. Redeemers, black codes
   c. voter fraud, poll tax
   d. white supremacy, Holocaust
   e. separate but equal, *Plessy* v. *Ferguson*
   f. vigilante justice, lynching

4. After Mark Twain read *Southern Horrors* by Ida B. Wells, he wrote an essay entitled "The United States of Lynchdom." Pretend you are Twain. Write your own opening paragraph for his essay protesting mob murders.

5. Imagine you are one of the students at Tuskegee Institute. Both Booker T. Washington and George Washington Carver are among your teachers. Write a letter to a friend describing your studies.

6. The author named the chapter about Booker T. Washington, "A Man and His Times." Why do you think she chose this title?

7. The author named the chapter about W. E. B. DuBois, "A Man Ahead of His Times." Why do you think she chose this title?

8. Booker T. Washington wrote: "No race can prosper till it learns that there is as much dignity in tilling fields as in writing a poem. It is at the bottom of life that we must begin, and not at the top." How might W. E. B. DuBois react to this statement?

9. **Thinking About the Big Ideas**   Reread the dissenting, or minority, opinion of Justice John Marshall Harlan in *Plessy* v. *Ferguson*. How would Justice Harlan define *justice*?

10. **Thinking About the Big Ideas**   If you were an African American in the late 1800s, what changes would have to be made so that your children could enjoy the promise of equal justice for all?

RESOURCE PAGE 1

Readmission of Former Confederate States to the Union

Directions: The map shows the years that the former Confederate states were readmitted to the Union. It also shows the Military Districts that governed the South during Reconstruction. Study the map, and then follow your teacher's directions.

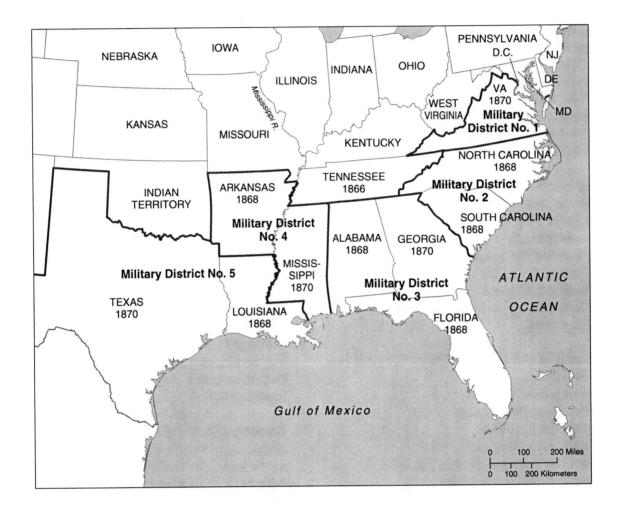

RESOURCE PAGE 2

The Freedmen's Third Reader

Directions: Congress created the Freedmen's Bureau to help people freed from slavery. In addition to food, clothing, and shelter, the Freedmen's Bureau opened schools. Below is an excerpt from the *Freedmen's Third Reader,* a book used in many of those schools. Read the excerpt. Then answer the questions that follow.

Note

This *Third Reader* is believed to be adapted to the wants of the Freedmen in the following particulars:

1. It contains elementary instruction in respect to the history and government of our country.
2. It contains interesting biographies of colored persons.
3. It presents to the Freedmen the life and words of Abraham Lincoln.…

Lesson XXXIX

1. Phillis Wheatley…was brought to this country from Africa in the year 1761. She was then between seven and eight years old. She was bought by Mrs. John Wheatley, a Boston lady..
2. Phillis early showed great eagerness for learning.…
3. She was treated by her mistress more as a child than a slave, and not only allowed, but encouraged, to study. Many persons of learning took great interest in her, and helped her.…
4. Phillis was very fond of reading and writing poetry. At one time, General [George] Washington, having received some lines from her, replied by a letter, in which he says, "I thank you most sincerely for your polite notice of me in the elegant lines you enclosed," and tells her he would be happy to see her should she ever come to Cambridge, where his "headquarters" then were.
5. At the age of nineteen…with a member of the Wheatley family she visited England, and was well received by many distinguished persons. While there, her poems were published. She returned to America, where she died in her twenty-sixth year.

Source: The American Tract Society, 1866.

---

1. Read the "Note." Explain why the contents of the *Reader* would meet "the wants of the Freedmen."

   _____

   _____

2. Why do you think a biography of Phillis Wheatley was included in *The Freedmen's Third Reader?*

   _____

   _____

3. What do you think the effect of the story was on freedmen and freedwomen who were finally able to get an education?

   _____

   _____

RESOURCE PAGE 3

Civil Rights in Alabama, 1874

Directions: The document describes some of the grievances of black citizens of Alabama in 1874. Read the document. Then answer the questions that follow.

House of Representatives, 43rd Congress, 2nd Session
A memorial of a convention of colored citizens assembled in the city of Montgomery, Ala., on December 2, 1874.

December 22, 1874.—Referred to a select Committee on Alabama affairs and ordered to be printed.

To the Speaker of the House of Representatives:
I have the honor to transmit herewith, for the information of Congress, a memorial forwarded to me by a convention of colored citizens assembled in the city of Montgomery, Ala., on the 2d of this month.
U.S. GRANT [President]   EXECUTIVE MANSION, December 22, 1874.

To His Excellency the President of the United States, and the honorable the Congress of the United States:
The colored people of the State of Alabama, who by virtue of the three latest amendments to the Constitution of the United States became emancipated, and also became citizens of the United States, feeling anxiously and solemnly impressed by their past and present condition in the State of Alabama, and by the grave and menacing dangers that now surround and threaten them and their constitutional rights, have as a race and as a people assembled together in convention to consider their situation, and to take solemn counsel together as to what it becomes them to do for their self-preservation….The most atrocious crimes committed against us by white men go unnoticed or unpunished. We can be killed, or our property destroyed, by white men, with utter impunity and safety to the criminal. If we commit any offense, punishment follows surely, quickly and vindictively….
The question which our case and condition presents to you is simply this: whether our constitutional rights as citizens are to be a reality or a mockery, a protection and a boon or a danger and a curse; whether we are to be freemen in fact or only in name; and whether the late amendments to the constitution are to be practically enforced or to become a nullity and stand only as "dead letters in the statute book…." We ask its [the U.S. government's] immediate interference in the terrible situation that it has left us after solemnly promising to guard us in the enjoyment of…all the rights of citizenship.

Source: House of Representatives, 43rd Congress, 2nd Session , Ex. Doc. No. 46

---

1. What prompted the convention of black citizens and this appeal?

_____

2. What action does the convention request from the president and Congress?

_____

3. Why do the black citizens of Alabama feel abandoned?

_____

4. Compare this document to the petition featured on page 43 of Book Seven. What are the similarities and differences? What action do you think was taken on behalf of black citizens of the South by the president or Congress in the 1870s?

_____

_____

RESOURCE PAGE 4

Songs of the West

Directions: "Whoopee Ti-Yi-Yo" was sung by cowboys in the late 1800s. A *dogie* is an orphaned calf or one abandoned by its mother; *cowpuncher* is another word for *cowboy*. "Drill, Ye Tarriers, Drill!" was sung by workers on the Union Pacific and other railroads in the late 1800s. A "tarrier" was a worker who worked beside steam drills moving rock. Read the two songs. Then answer the questions that follow.

Whoopee Ti-Yi-Yo
As I was walkin' one morning for pleasure,
I spied a cowpuncher a-lopin' along,
His hat was thrown back and his spurs were a-jinglin'
And as he approached he was singin' this song:

Whoopee ti-yi-yo, git along little dogies,
For you know Wyoming'll be your new home.

Whoopee ti-yi-yo, git along little dogies,
For you know that Wyoming'll be your new home.

Source: Margaret Bradford Boni,
The Fireside Book of Folk Songs. Simon and Schuster, 1947.

Drill, Ye Tarriers, Drill!
The new foreman was Jim McCann
By [gosh] he was a blame mean man!
Past week a premature blast went off
And a mile in the air went big Jim Goff.
When next pay day came around,
Jim Goff a dollar short was found;
When he asked, "What for?" came this reply,
"You're docked for the time you were up in the sky."

And, drill, ye tarriers, drill!
It's work all day
For sugar in your tay [tea];
Working on the U. Pay Railway
Drill, ye tarriers, drill!
And blast!
And fire!

Source: Meridel LeSueur,
American Folkways Series: North Star Country.
Duell, Sloane, and Pearce, 1945.

---

1. How did singing songs like these help railroad workers and cowboys do their jobs?

_____

_____

2. Why do think these songs became popular with people who were neither cowboys nor railroad workers?

_____

_____

3. What evidence of the dangers of working on the railroad can you find in "Drill, Ye Tarriers, Drill!" What does "Fire!" mean in the last line?

_____

_____

RESOURCE PAGE 5

Growth of Railroads, 1870-1890

Directions: The maps below show the growth of American railroads from 1870 to 1890. The table shows population in selected western cities in those years. Use the information to answer the questions that follow.

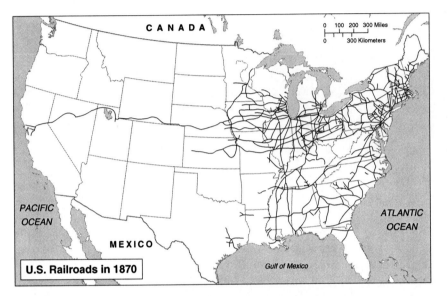

POPULATION OF WESTERN CITIES, 1870 AND 1890

City	1870	1890
Chicago, IL	298,977	1,099,850
Denver, CO	4,759	106,713
Detroit, MI	79,577	205,876
Kansas City, MO	32,260	132,716
Omaha, NE	16,083	140,452
St. Louis, MO	310,864	451,770
St. Paul, MN	20,030	133,156]

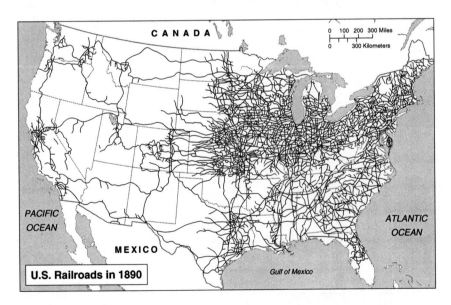

1. Use a political map of the United States to locate the cities listed in the table. Mark their locations on both maps on this page.
2. On a separate sheet of paper, write a paragraph in which you draw conclusions about the effects of the coming of the railroad on western cities.

RESOURCE PAGE 6

Chinese Exclusion Act (Excerpts)

Directions: In 1882, in response to mounting pressure from Americans who opposed Chinese immigration, Congress passed a law barring Chinese immigrants. Read the document. Then answer the questions that follow.

> WHEREAS, in the opinion of the Government of the United States the coming of Chinese laborers to this country endangers the good order of certain localities within the territory thereof: Therefore,
>
> Be it enacted, That from and after the expiration of ninety days after the passage of this act, and until the expiration of ten years next after the passage of this act, the coming of Chinese laborers to the United States be,…suspended; and during such suspension it shall not be lawful for any Chinese laborer to come, or, having so come after the expiration of said ninety days, to remain within the United States.…
>
> [SEC. 2: Provides for fine and imprisonment of anyone who brings a Chinese laborer to the United States by ship.]
>
> SEC 3. That the two foregoing sections shall not apply to Chinese laborers who were in the United States on the seventeenth day of November, eighteen hundred and eighty, or who shall have come into the same before the expiration of ninety days next after the passage of this act,…
>
> SEC. 14. That hereafter no State court or court of the United States shall admit Chinese to citizenship; and all laws in conflict with this act are hereby repealed.
>
> SEC 15. That the words "Chinese laborers," whenever used in this act shall be construed to mean both skilled and unskilled laborers and Chinese employed in mining.
>
> Source: Henry Steele Commager, *Documents of American History.* Appleton-Century-Crofts, 1968.

1. What reason is given for the act? Restate it in your own words.

_____

_____

2. From what you have read in Book Seven, who was "endangering the good order" of places where Chinese lived—the Chinese or people opposed to immigration?

_____

_____

3. How long is this act supposed to be in effect?

_____

_____

RESOURCE PAGE 7

The Advance of Women's Suffrage in America

Directions: The map below shows the years in which different states guaranteed women the right to vote. The states with no dates did not do so until after the 19th Amendment was ratified. Study the map and answer the questions.

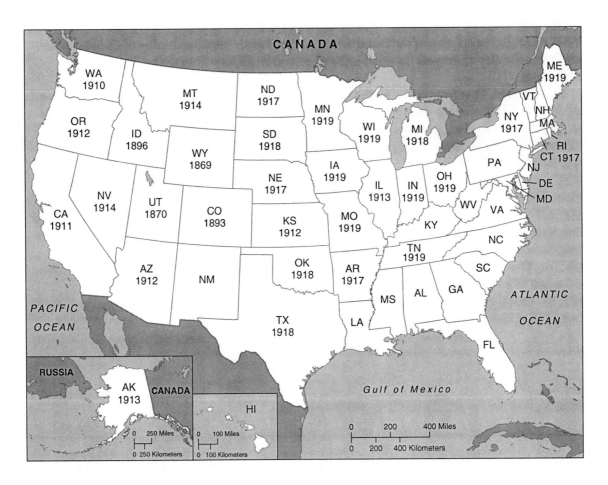

1. Name the states in which women could vote before 1900.

_____

2. The 19th Amendment passed Congress in 1919. How many states had granted women the right to vote by then?

_____

3. In which part of the country were most of the states that allowed women to vote early on?

_____

4. List possible reasons why these states allowed women to vote well before the 19th Amendment was ratified.

_____

_____

RESOURCE PAGE 8

Civil Government Pupil's Examination, June 1897

Directions: The following examination given by teacher Estelle Moger to students in the Brooklyn, New York public schools in 1897 was found 100 years later in a wooden chest in her nephew's attic. Read the examination, and then answer the questions that follow.

I.	What is the right of suffrage? Name classes wholly or partly deprived of it.
II.	What determines the number of votes a state casts for President? How many has this state?
III.	What is meant by a majority vote; a plurality vote?
IV.	Mention the duties of a constable. Is he a township, county or state officer?
V.	Distinguish between a direct and indirect tax. Give examples.
VI.	Distinguish between the duties of a petit and a grand jury.
VII.	Why should people who have no children be taxed to support the public schools?
VIII.	What is the duty of the U.S. Government to each state in respect to (a) form of government, (b) invasion, (c) insurrection?
IX.	Mention 2 provisions in the constitution that were the result of a compromise.
X.	What constitutes the legislative body of (a) a city, (b) of a county?

Source: Moger family papers

1. Many of the pupils in Brooklyn schools in 1897 were not yet citizens of the United States. Explain why they would be studying information about civil government?

_____

2. Explain why the answer to the first question would have changed after 1920.

3. Research the answer to the second question for your state.

_____

RESOURCE PAGE 9

Excerpt from *Southern Horrors* by Ida B. Wells

Directions: In 1892 Ida B. Wells, the outspoken champion of rights for black Americans, published *Southern Horrors: Lynch Law in All Its Phases*. The book was a blistering exposé of crimes against black people. Wells was living in Chicago in 1892, having been forced to move north after her newspaper office in Memphis, Tennessee, was destroyed by a mob. Read the excerpt. Then answer the questions that follow.

One by one the Southern States have legally(?) disfranchised the Afro-American, and since the repeal of the Civil Rights Bill nearly every Southern State has passed separate [railroad] car laws with a penalty against their infringement....All this while, although the political cause has been removed, the butcheries of black men at Barnwell, S.C., Carrolton, Miss., Waycross, Ga., and Memphis, Tenn., have gone on; also the flaying alive of a man in Kentucky, the burning of one in Arkansas, the hanging of a fifteen-year-old girl in Louisiana, a woman in Jackson, Tenn., and one in Hollendale, Miss., until the dark and bloody record of the South shows 728 Afro-Americans lynched during the past 8 years. Not 50 of these were for political causes, the rest were for all manner of accusations from that of rape of white women, to the case of the boy Will Lewis who was hanged at Tullahoma, Tenn., last year for being drunk and "sassy" to white folks....

These statistics compiled by the Chicago "Tribune" were given the first of this year (1892). Since then, not less than one hundred and fifty have been known to have met violent death at the hands of cruel bloodthirsty mobs during the past nine months....

Men who stand high in the esteem of the public...stand as cowards who fear to open their mouths before this great outrage. They do not see that by their tacit encouragement, their silent acquiescence, the black shadow of lawlessness in the form of lynch law is spreading its wings over the whole country....

The mob spirit has grown....It has left the out-of-the-way places where ignorance prevails, has thrown off the mask and with this new cry stalks in broad daylight in large cities, the centers of civilization, and is encouraged by the "leading citizens" and the press.

Source: Judith Papachristou, *Women Together: A History in Documents of the Women's Movement in the United States.* Alfred A. Knopf, 1976.

1. How would you describe the tone of Wells's writing?

_____

2. What shocked you? Do you think it would have shocked people in 1892?

_____

_____

3. Who does the author believe is encouraging "lynch law"?

_____

4. What question would you have asked Wells if you had met her in 1892?

_____

USING THE MAP RESOURCE PAGES

These maps are provided for use with class projects and activities:

Reproducible U.S. Relief map*

Project suggestion: Use the map with the ongoing "Using Maps" project suggested on TG page 30. Have students create an overview of the migrations and population shift described in Reconstructing America by charting movements of peoples as they read the book.

Reproducible Blank U.S. Political map*

Project suggestion: Use this map as an alternate to the U.S. relief map for the Geography Connections activity on TG page 34, described above.

Also, use this map for the "Using Maps" activity on TG page 85. Have students trace state outlines to make a map of the United States at the time of the Centennial in 1876.

In addition, use this map for the "Interpreting Historical Maps" activity on TG page 92. Have students color and label the map to describe location and number of lynchings and hate crimes during Reconstruction.

Reproducible Western U.S. Relief map*

Project suggestion: Use this map for the "Battle for the West" project described on TG pages 51-52 and throughout Part 3. Have students create and label a map of important boundaries, trails, cities, landforms and events as they read about the settlement of the West.

* These maps are also printed in each Student Study Guide for *Reconstructing America*.

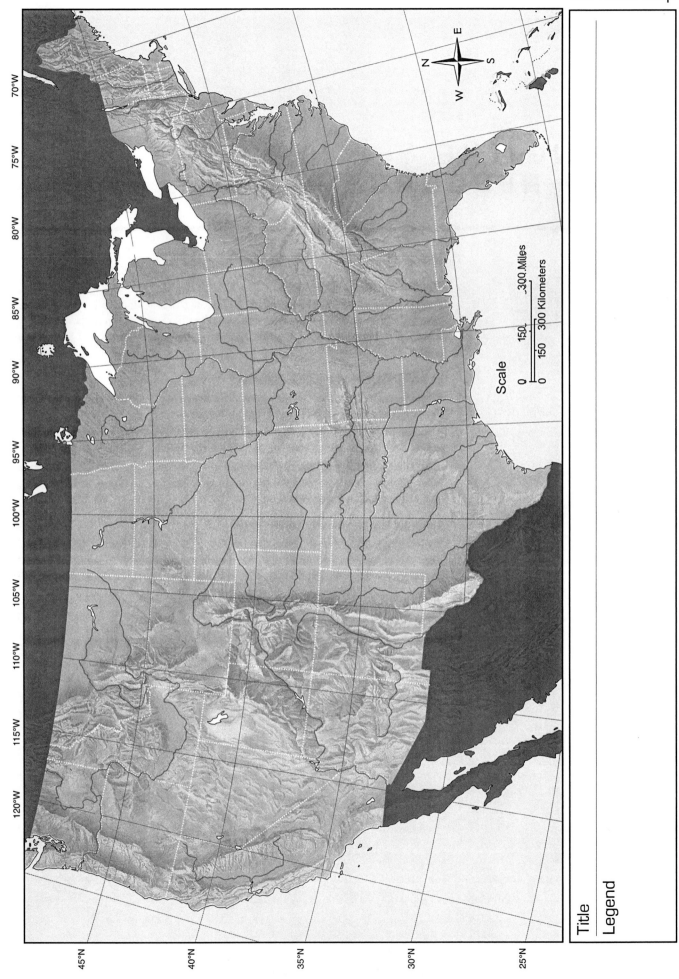

Title

Legend

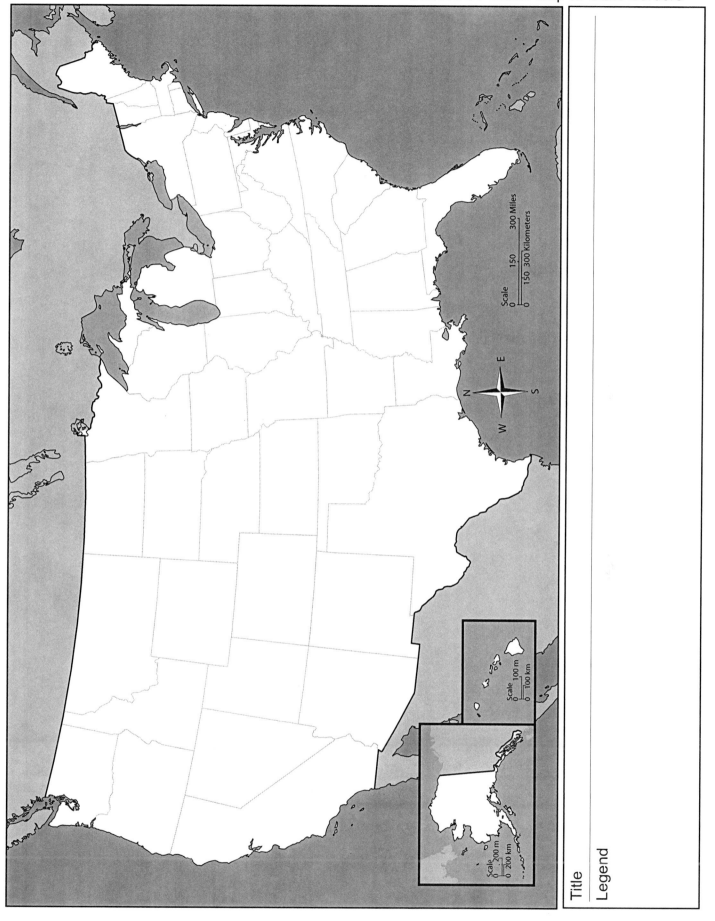

Scale
0   150   300 Miles
0   150   300 Kilometers

N
W   E
S

Scale
0   100 m
0   100 km

Scale
0   200 m
0   200 km

Title

Legend

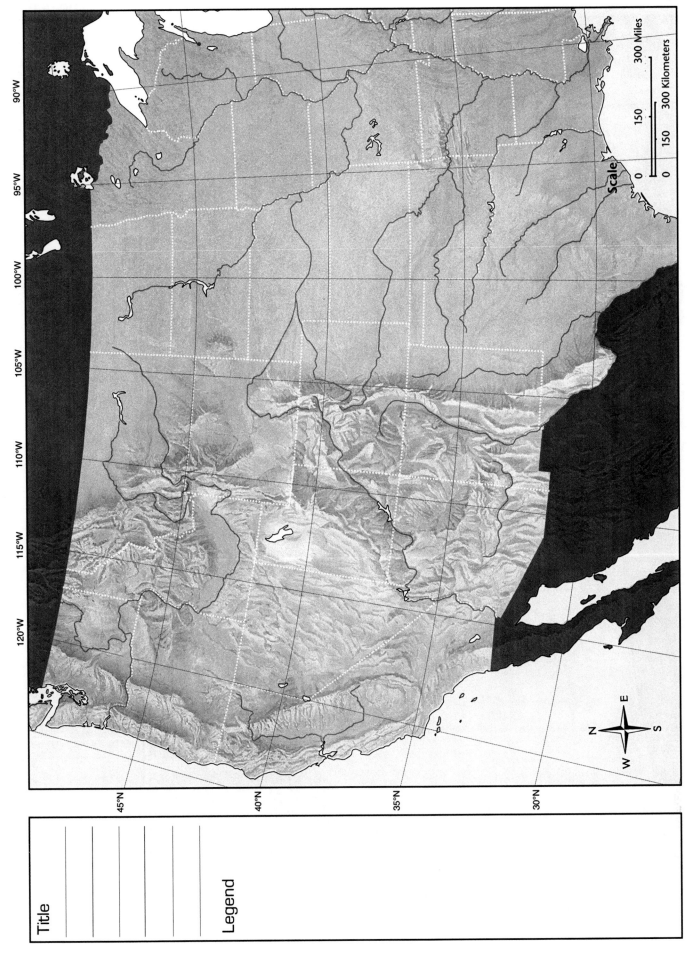

Scale

300 Miles

150

0

300 Kilometers

150

0

90°W

95°W

100°W

105°W

110°W

115°W

120°W

45°N

40°N

35°N

30°N

N

E

W

S

Title

Legend

SCORING RUBRIC

The reproducibles on the following pages have been adapted from this rubric for use as handouts and a student self-scoring activity, with added focus on planning, cooperation, revision and presentation. You may wish to tailor the self-scoring activity—for example, asking students to comment on how low scores could be improved, or focusing only on specific rubric points. Use the Library/Media Center Research Log to help students focus and evaluate their research for projects and assignments.

As with any rubric, you should introduce and explain the rubric before students begin their assignments. The more thoroughly your students understand how they will be evaluated, the better prepared they will be to produce projects that fulfill your expectations.

	ORGANIZATION	CONTENT	ORAL/WRITTEN CONVENTIONS	GROUP PARTICIPATION
4	• Clearly addresses all parts of the writing task. • Demonstrates a clear understanding of purpose and audience. • Maintains a consistent point of view, focus, and organizational structure, including the effective use of transitions. • Includes a clearly presented central idea with relevant facts, details, and/or explanations.	• Demonstrates that the topic was well researched. • Uses only information that was essential and relevant to the topic. • Presents the topic thoroughly and accurately. • Reaches reasonable conclusions clearly based on evidence.	• Contains few, if any, errors in grammar, punctuation, capitalization, or spelling. • Uses a variety of sentence types. • Speaks clearly, using effective volume and intonation.	• Demonstrated high levels of participation and effective decision making. • Planned well and used time efficiently. • Demonstrated ability to negotiate opinions fairly and reach compromise when needed. • Utilized effective visual aids.
3	• Addresses all parts of the writing task. • Demonstrates a general understanding of purpose and audience. • Maintains a mostly consistent point of view, focus, and organizational structure, including the effective use of some transitions. • Presents a central idea with mostly relevant facts, details, and/or explanations.	• Demonstrates that the topic was sufficiently researched. • Uses mainly information that was essential and relevant to the topic. • Presents the topic accurately but leaves some aspects unexplored. • Reaches reasonable conclusions loosely related to evidence.	• Contains some errors in grammar, punctuation, capitalization, or spelling. • Uses a variety of sentence types. • Speaks somewhat clearly, using effective volume and intonation.	• Demonstrated good participation and decision making with few distractions. • Planning and used its time acceptably. • Demonstrated ability to negotiate opinions and compromise with little aggression or unfairness.
2	• Addresses only parts of the writing task. • Demonstrates little understanding of purpose and audience. • Maintains an inconsistent point of view, focus, and/or organizational structure, which may include ineffective or awkward transitions that do not unify important ideas. • Suggests a central idea with limited facts, details, and/or explanations.	• Demonstrates that the topic was minimally researched. • Uses a mix of relevant and irrelevant information. • Presents the topic with some factual errors and leaves some aspects unexplored. • Reaches conclusions that do not stem from evidence presented in the project.	• Contains several errors in grammar, punctuation, capitalization, or spelling. These errors may interfere with the reader's understanding of the writing. • Uses little variety in sentence types. • Speaks unclearly or too quickly. May interfere with the audience's understanding of the project.	• Demonstrated uneven participation or was often off-topic. Task distribution was lopsided. • Did not show a clear plan for the project, and did not use time well. • Allowed one or two opinions to dominate the activity, or had trouble reaching a fair consensus.
1	• Addresses only one part of the writing task. • Demonstrates no understanding of purpose and audience. • Lacks a point of view, focus, organizational structure, and transitions that unify important ideas. • Lacks a central idea but may contain marginally related facts, details, and/or explanations.	• Demonstrates that the topic was poorly researched. • Does not discriminate relevant from irrelevant information. • Presents the topic incompletely, with many factual errors. • Did not reach conclusions.	• Contains serious errors in grammar, punctuation, capitalization, or spelling. These errors interfere with the reader's understanding of the writing. • Uses no sentence variety. • Speaks unclearly. The audience must struggle to understand the project.	• Demonstrated poor participation by the majority of the group. Tasks were completed by a small minority. • Failed to show planning or effective use of time. • Was dominated by a single voice, or allowed hostility to derail the project.

NAME _____   **PROJECT** _____

DATE _____

ORGANIZATION & FOCUS	CONTENT	ORAL/WRITTEN CONVENTIONS	GROUP PARTICIPATION

COMMENTS AND SUGGESTIONS

UNDERSTANDING YOUR SCORE

Organization: Your project should be clear, focused on a main idea, and organized. You should use details and facts to support your main idea.

Content: You should use strong research skills. Your project should be thorough and accurate.

Oral/Written Conventions: For writing projects, you should use good composition, grammar, punctuation, and spelling, with a good variety of sentence types. For oral projects, you should engage the class using good public speaking skills.

Group Participation: Your group should cooperate fairly and use its time well to plan, assign and revise the tasks involved in the project.

NAME _____ **GROUP MEMBERS** _____

_____

_____

_____

Use this worksheet to describe your project by finishing the sentences below. For individual projects and writing assignments, use the "How I did" section. For group projects, use both "How I did" and "How we did" sections.

The purpose of this project is to :

```
┌─────────────────────────────────────────────────────────────┐
│                                                             │
│                                                             │
│                                                             │
│                                                             │
└─────────────────────────────────────────────────────────────┘
```

Scoring Key =   **4** – extremely well
3 – well
2 – could have been better
1 – not well at all

HOW I DID

I understood the purpose and requirements for this project...

I planned and organized my time and work...

This project showed clear organization that emphasized the central idea...

I supported my point with details and description...

I polished and revised this project...

I utilized correct grammar and good writing/speaking style...

Overall, this project met its purpose...

HOW WE DID

We divided up tasks...

We cooperated and listened to each other...

We talked through what we didn't understand...

We used all our time to make this project the best it could be...

Overall, as a group we worked together...

I contributed and cooperated with the team...

LIBRARY/ MEDIA CENTER RESEARCH LOG

NAME _____

DUE DATE _____

Brainstorm: Other Sources and Places to Look

Places I **Know** to Look

What I Need to **Find**

I need to use:
- ☐ primary sources.
- ☐ secondary

WHAT I FOUND

Title/Author/Location (call # or URL)

	Book/Periodical	Website	Other	Primary Source	Secondary Source	Suggestion	Library Catalog	Browsing	Internet Search	Web link	helpful	relevant
	☐	☐	☐	☐	☐	☐	☐	☐	☐	☐		
	☐	☐	☐	☐	☐	☐	☐	☐	☐	☐		
	☐	☐	☐	☐	☐	☐	☐	☐	☐	☐		
	☐	☐	☐	☐	☐	☐	☐	☐	☐	☐		
	☐	☐	☐	☐	☐	☐	☐	☐	☐	☐		
	☐	☐	☐	☐	☐	☐	☐	☐	☐	☐		
	☐	☐	☐	☐	☐	☐	☐	☐	☐	☐		

How I Found it

Rate each source from 1 (low) to 4 (high) in the categories below

OUTLINE

MAIN IDEA: _____
_____
_____

DETAIL: _____
_____

DETAIL: _____
_____

DETAIL: _____
_____

MAIN IDEA: _____
_____
_____

DETAIL: _____
_____

DETAIL: _____
_____

DETAIL: _____
_____

Name _____ Date _____

MAIN IDEA MAP

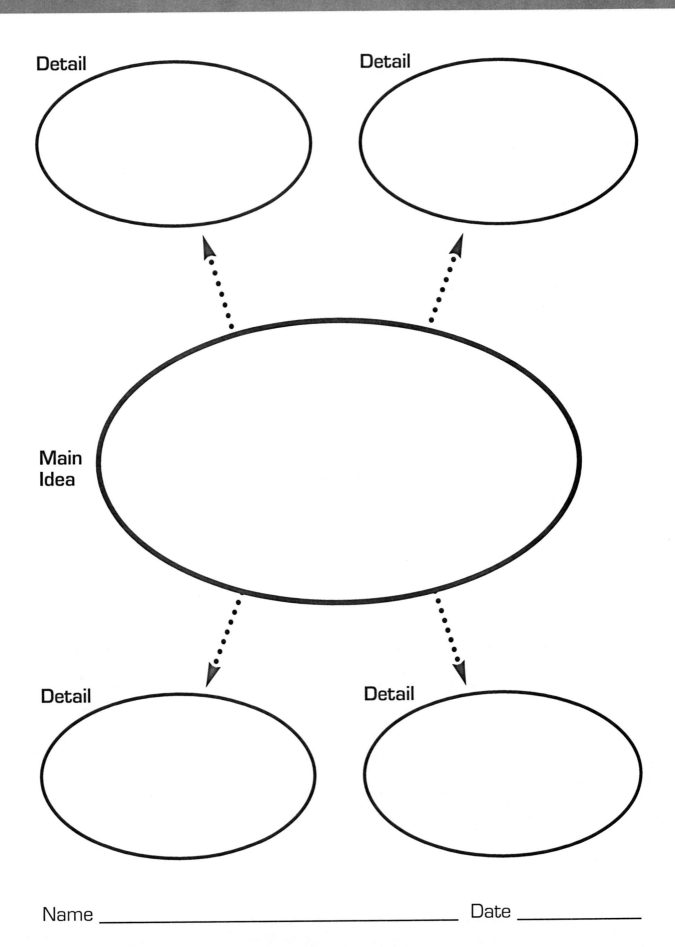

Detail

Detail

Main Idea

Detail

Detail

Name _____ Date _____

K-W-L CHART

K	W	L
What I Know	What I Want to Know	What I Learned

Name _____ Date _____

VENN DIAGRAM

Write differences in the circles. Write similarities where the circles overlap.

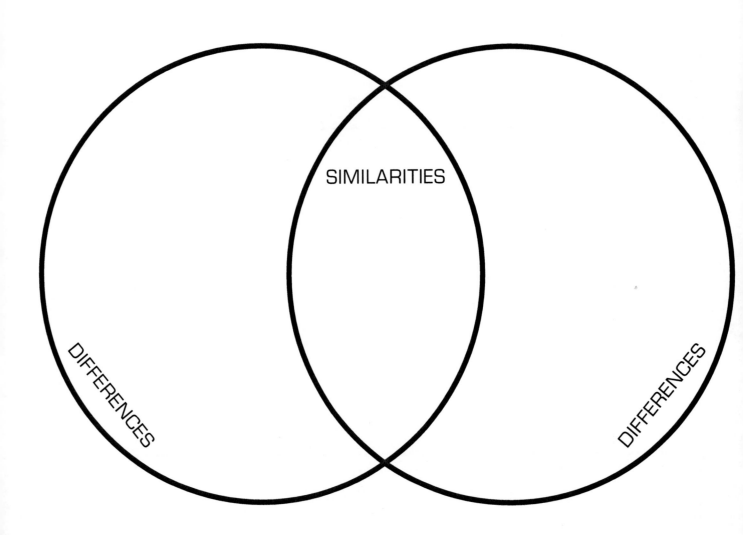

SIMILARITIES

DIFFERENCES

DIFFERENCES

Name _____ Date _____

TIMELINE

DATE

EVENT Draw lines to connect the event to the correct year on the timeline.

Name _____ Date

SEQUENCE OF EVENTS CHART

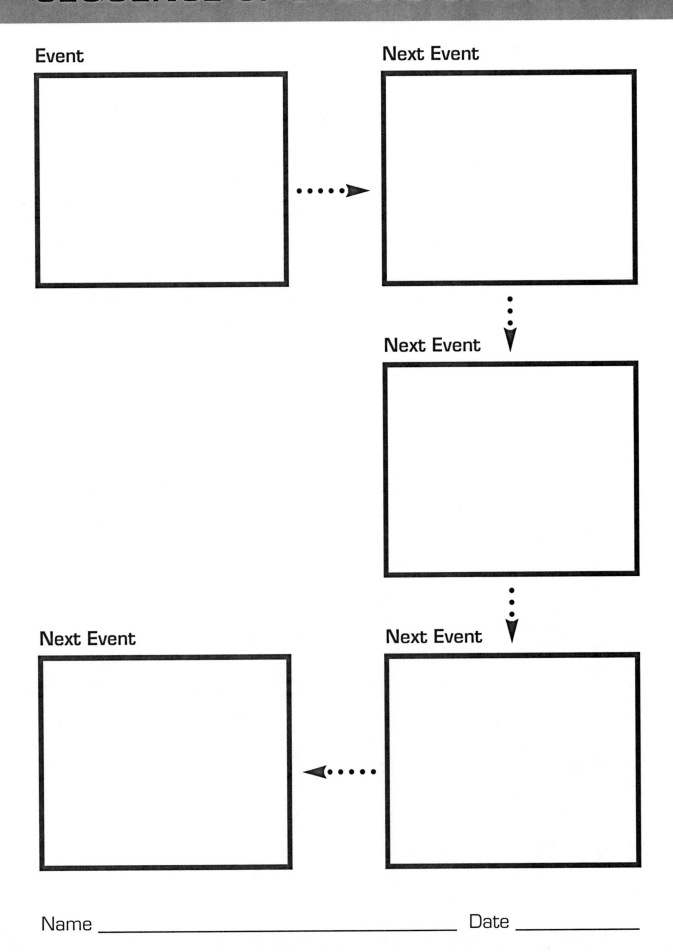

Event

Next Event

Next Event

Next Event

Next Event

Name _____ Date _____

T–CHART

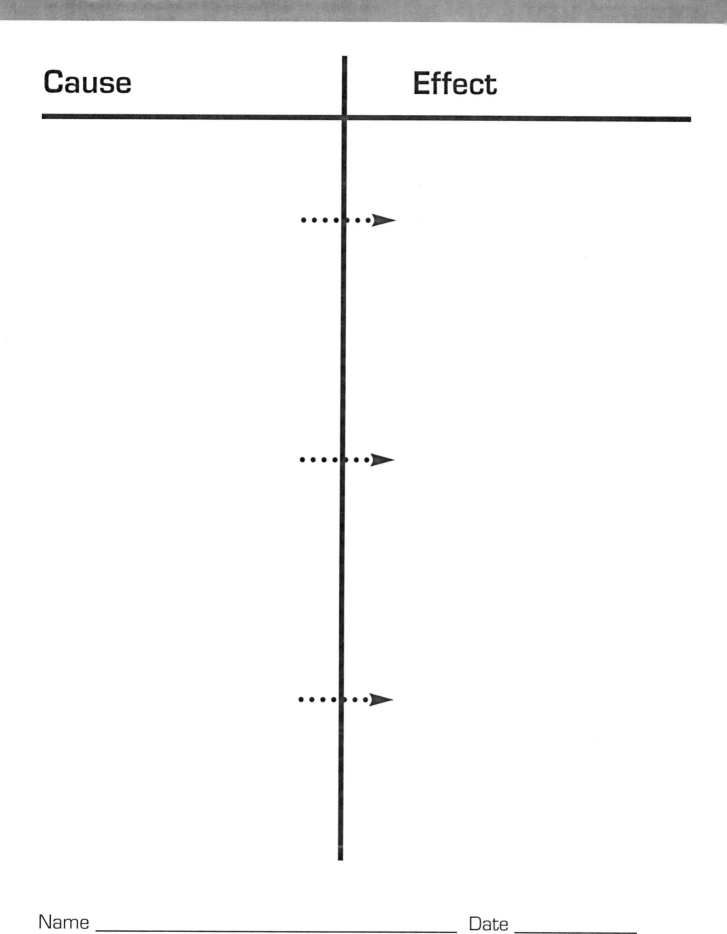

Cause | Effect

Name _____ Date _____

TEACHING GUIDE
ANSWER KEY

CHECK-UP 1

1. (a) wanted to make it easy for the country to reunite but died before his ideas could be implemented (b) believed the States would protect freedmen's rights (c) founded a school for black Virginians (d) went South to teach former slaves (e-f) black Senators from Mississippi (g) believed federal government had to enforce Reconstruction in the South (h) Senator who cast vote against impeaching President Johnson, saving him from conviction

2. (a) physical destruction, displaced people (b) race riots (c) instruction of former slaves (d) economic activity of the "New South"

3. organization dedicated to educating and protecting the civil rights of freedmen and freedwomen; established schools, provided food and clothing (b) rule by armed forces; enforced Congressional Reconstruction (c) years when U.S. Army enforced Congressional reconstruction (d) Northerners who went south after the Civil War; some helped; some were profiteers and all aroused hatred among some Southerners (e) Southerners who cooperated with Northerners during Reconstruction; widely disliked; (f) Congress' right to try the President for "high crimes and misdemeanors"

4. through immigration and through the purchase of Alaska

5. (a) terrorized blacks who sought to exercise their rights (b) limited the legal rights of blacks and imposed segregation (c) exposed blacks and whites to violence and murder

6. Former Confederate states had to write a new constitution modeled on the U.S. Constitution that allowed all males over 21 to vote except former Confederate soldiers and criminals (a) might have supported them because of new economic and political opportunities for Northerners who headed into the South (b) probably supported them because Northerners gave scalawags a role in government (c) probably supported them because of increased political rights (d) probably opposed them because of restricted political role and new opportunities extended to blacks

7. Arguments should focus on Johnson's support of states' rights, willingness to allow former Confederates to resume power, unwillingness to use federal power to guarantee liberty and justice to black Southerners.

8. Students may conclude it was fair because the vote was very close, all Senators took part, and the vote took place under public scrutiny.

9. Obituaries will vary, but most black Americans regarded Stevens as a hero and a champion of liberty.

10. 14th Amendment: guaranteed that no state could unjustly infringe upon liberties guaranteed by the Constitution; limited states' rights by giving the Supreme Court the power to declare state laws unconstitutional; gave the Supreme Court the ability to uphold citizens' right to "due process of law" threatened by state laws.

CHECK-UP 2

1. (a) a black Congressman who pushed for civil rights legislation to protect freedmen (b) a black minister, "the most cultured man" at the Florida constitutional convention (c) daughter of the black owner of Jefferson Davis's former home; forced to leave when Davis was allowed to claim it (d) former President of the Confederacy, pardoned by President Johnson (e) his corrupt Presidential administration led to economic chaos and the end of Reconstruction (f) elected governor of South Carolina with the help of violent supporters; blacks had the vote as long as he was governor (g) agreed to pull federal troops out of the South if blacks were treated fairly; his election spelled the end of Reconstruction

2. (a) site of the South Carolina constitutional convention (b) prison where Jefferson Davis was held after the end of the Civil War (c) former plantation of Jefferson Davis; bought by Benjamin Montgomery who founded a self-sufficient black community until Davis was allowed to reclaim it (d) black community founded by Isaiah Montgomery in 1887

3. (a) economic system that kept black Southerners indebted to whites (b) tax imposed on black voters (c) murder of black people by whites as part of a campaign to keep black Southerners from exercising their rights (d) separation of the races, enforced by law in the South at the end of Reconstruction (e) members of Democratic party who regained power in the South and refused to allow black Southerners their rights

4. the people of different races who attended the meeting

5. Advertisements should highlight the right to enjoy the profits of one's own labor and the right of African American members of the community to elect their own officials.

6. Students will probably note that the Montgomery family legally bought the land. The fact that Davis won his claim reveals the disregard for black rights in courts of law.

7. for his inability to enforce Reconstruction or to curb corruption within his own government

8. By abolishing slavery the 13th Amendment gave all constitutional rights to African Americans. (a) The 15th Amendment guaranteed universal manhood suffrage to blacks. Poll taxes restricted that right. (a-c) The 14th Amendment guaranteed "due process of law" and "equal protection of the laws." The intent of both poll taxes and segregated railroad cars refused blacks these rights. Lynchings clearly violated the "due process" clause, by executing people without benefit of a trial.

9. Dr. Martin Luther King, Jr.

10. Reconstruction legislatures allowed black voters and politicians to take part in the political process. They financed public education, roads, and other public works, all of which are part of our lives today.

CHECK-UP 3

1. (a) geologist who explored the Grand Canyon (b) African American inventor who held 75 patents (c) cattle buyer in Abilene who spurred the Texas longhorn cattle drives (d) cattleman who mapped the cattle trail from Texas to Abilene named for him (e) African American cowboy known as Deadwood Dick (f) cowgirl who made millions in the cattle business (g) railroad tycoon; represented Central Pacific Railroad at the ceremony completing the transcontinental railroad (h) builder of fancy railroad cars and "sleepers" with seats that converted into beds; known as a "welfare capitalist" (i) author who captured the immigrant experience and life of farmers on the Plains (j) businessman and inventor; manufacture of his reaper brought industrial revo-

lution to agriculture (k) African American scientist who developed hundreds of ways to use peanuts and other foods (l) Sioux warrior who defeated Custer (m) eloquent leader of the Nez Perce whose attempted flight to avoid being removed to a reservation brought attention to the plight of Native Americans

2. (a) final land rush onto Native American lands (b) meeting place of the eastward and westward sections of the transcontinental railroad; trains carried buffalo hunters and settlers west onto Native American lands (c) site of battle that ended with Native Americans' defeat of General Custer (d) reservation school that taught Native Americans American ways (e) site of massacre that marked the end of the Indian wars for the West.

3. (a) money used to buy land on the Great Plains (b) tough breed of Texas cattle, driven north to market by cowboys (c) the wooden cross pieces that support railroad rails; used in building the railroads that opened the West (d) money provided by government to help build railroads (e) basic railroad car, uncomfortable but cheap transport; many people could afford to travel by train (f) permitted qualified people to buy 160 acres of public land for $10; encouraged immigrants and others to settle the Great Plains (g) twisted wire with sharp points; made it possible to fence large areas on the prairie which led to clashes between farmers and cattle drivers (h) grasslands with soil that is difficult to plow (i) provided land grants to states to establish agricultural colleges (j) unwanted land allotted to Indians

4. Native Americans saw the land as their ancestral homeland and territory granted to them by treaty. They saw it as free, open land suitable for hunting. Homesteaders saw the Plains as wild land to be tamed for farming.

5. hardships: weather, stampedes, thirst, rustlers, hostile Indians; benefits: freedom and independence.

6. Telegrams should cite reasons for the event's importance such as the linking of East and West and the geographic and engineering difficulties overcome by the builders.

7. Ads should touch on the benefit to farmers in being able to protect their crops and animals and in keeping cattle drives off their land

8. fertility of the land, low cost of land, and the open, flat spaces that made it possible to use large machinery such as the reaper

9. justice: the application of the same liberties, laws, and government to all people.

10. Native Americans: injustices and loss of a way of life; nation: extraordinary growth as a result of settlement; expansion of transportation; the rise of commercial farming.

CHECK-UP 4

1. (a) schemer—corrupt political boss in New York City, used his power to get money for himself (b) dreamer—built subway to improve traffic congestion in New York City (c) schemer—member of Tammany Hall political machine in New York City (d) dreamer—attacked Boss Tweed and corruption through powerful cartoons (e) both—promoter, entertainer, huckster (f) dreamer—author who captured Americans' dreams and problems with humor and honesty

2. (a) East, crowded, polluted (b) Midwest, quiet town on Mississippi River; riverboat stop (c) West, rich, "literary capital of the West" (d) West, booming mining town

3. (a) dishonest money collected by corrupt politicians (b) powerful urban political machine in New York City (c) unofficial governments that helped people for a price (d) people a politician represents (e) deception and swindling (f) hoax or impostor (g) businessmen who fought each other and robbed everyone else (h) people who tried to make the country better (i) period of "glitter and gaudiness" and "ridiculous excess" when rich people spent money to show off

4. (a) that Tweed controlled the voting, thus undermining democracy (b) Beach built a subway "under his nose"; Nast drew cartoons exposing the corruption.

5. dishonest graft: blackmailers, gamblers, saloonkeepers, disorderly people. honest graft: making a profit off inside political deals. Both open government to corruption.

6. Students should use colorful language and descriptions of "rare spectacles," such as Jumbo, trapeze artists and human curiosities.

7. Answers will vary. Students should cite examples such as *Huckleberry Finn* in which the characters are a slave searching for freedom and a boy who loves adventure.

8. To encourage discussion, ask students what differences they see between how children and adults think. What advantages and disadvantages are there to each way of thinking?

9. Political machines, because they developed a power base and government outside of legitimate political channels.

CHECK-UP 5

1. (a) immigrant who became an ambassador and a Senator, a reformer who believed in ideals of Declaration of Independence and Constitution (b) Danish immigrant whose photographs of the poor helped get laws passed to improve conditions (c) sheriff in San Francisco who enforced a law unfairly, violating the rights of Chinese laundry owners (d) Chinese laundry owner who fought against discrimination and for equal rights by appealing his conviction to the Supreme Court (e) first woman justice of the peace who influenced men of both parties to vote for women's suffrage in Wyoming (f) headed an organization opposed to women's suffrage (g) leader of women's suffrage movement who, when arrested for voting illegally, refused to pay her fine to call attention to the injustice of denying votes to women (h) newspaperman and politician opposed to women's suffrage (i) woman who demanded right to practice law, ran for president, believed in equal rights

2. (a) site where immigrants were checked before entering the U.S. and where people from all over the world took first steps onto American soil (b) town where Ku Klux Klan started; opposed diversity (c) Chinese immigrants settling in San Francisco were discriminated against and attacked by nativists (d) the first territory (and then state) to permit women to vote and encourage diversity of voters (e) hometown of Susan B. Anthony; place where she tested the 15th amendment

3. (a) overcrowded apartment buildings with cheap rents where immigrants could afford to live, (b) area below decks on a steamship where poor immigrants traveled cheaply (c) name Chinese had for America; signified wealth available here compared to China (d) anti-Chinese movement in California that directly affected immigrants (e) law that denied Chinese immigrants entry to the U.S. (f) people who aren't citizens; Supreme Court ruled in *Yick Wo* v. *Hopkins* that aliens are entitled to equal protection of the laws

4. Immigration reached an all-time high; immigrants came from new regions, especially Central and Eastern Europe.

5. conditions such as overcrowded housing, polluted cities, discrimination, unfamiliar language

6. The law was applied unfairly (no male white laundry owners were arrested).

7. Lee Yick: equal protection of the laws, guaranteed in 14th Amendment, applies to aliens as well as citizens; Susan B. Anthony: challenged the 15th amendment that says all citizens can vote

8. Students should keep in mind the six reporter's questions: *Who? What? When? Where? Why? How?*

9. Monologues will vary, but should cite beliefs consistent with Antin's autobiographical statements and her age.

10. Answers will vary, but students should understand that belief in ideals such as liberty and equality motivated people to come to America and is the thread that holds the American people together.

CHECK-UP 6

1. (a) raised money for Centennial Exposition and Women's Building that featured work by women (b) built world's largest machine; symbolized American technology (c) inventor of the telephone, a wonder of American technology (d) leading women reformer who read Declaration of the Rights of Women at the Centennial reminding Americans there was still work to be done (e)Yale football coach who helped make football an American sport (f) America's most gifted and famous inventor; brought electric light to cities (g) lawyer whose financial backing and promotion of Edison helped bring electric light to New York City

2. (a) site of the Centennial Exposition which featured signs of progress in all areas (b) site of the first modern research laboratory set up by Thomas Edison and his assistants; inventions there included the first inexpensive light bulb (c) first city to be lit by electric lights

3. (a) one-hundredth anniversary; Centennial Exposition celebrated America's first 100 years (b) big public exhibition; Centennial Exposition celebrated 100 years of America (c) self-government, the principle on which the United States is based (d) goods sent out of the nation; in 1876 U.S. exports were greater than imports (e) people who are not rich and not poor; lived better in U.S. at the end of 19th century than ever before in history (f) material that glows inside electric light bulb; Edison discovered a practical filament and made electric light affordable

4. Speeches will vary, but they will probably emphasize positive achievements.

5. Students should mention specific displays, such as the telephone and Corliss steam engine.

6. that the ways of life between two classes vary dramatically

7. Most people at the time expressed shock, then anger.

8. In the ad students should mention qualities that might make a successful inventor.

9. that genius results from a lot of hard work

10. The changes mentioned should focus on technological advancements.

CHECK-UP 7

1. (a) challenged law about "separate but equal" (segregated) seating on railway cars which resulted in Supreme Court ruling that "separate but equal" was constitutional (b) only Supreme Court Justice to dissent in *Plessy* v. *Ferguson,* argued that the Constitution is colorblind (c) challenged segregation but lost in court, collected statistics and published information about lynching, never stopped fighting for justice (d) a national hero among whites because he believed that in order for blacks to have political power and social equality they first needed economic power, educated many black students at Tuskegee (e) writer and intellectual who spoke out in favor of full equality and against Washington's ideas, one of the founders of the NAACP, an organization dedicated to fighting injustice

2. (a) birthplace of Ida B. Wells, small town where blacks and whites lived in racial harmony (b) location of Hampton Institute, a college for African Americans attended by Booker T. Washington (c) location of Tuskegee Institute, which under Washington became prestigious African American college, training students in science, engineering, as well as practical skills like shoemaking (d) hometown of W. E. B. DuBois; place where he learned about democracy from attending town meetings (e) location of a meeting of black Americans, including W. E. B. Dubois, who announced they were working for civil rights for all

3. (a) name of character in a song; came to stand for policy of racial segregation (b) southern Democrats; passed laws similar to earlier black codes, depriving black Southerners of their rights and ending Reconstruction (c) both are ways of depriving black Southerners of voting power (d) the Holocaust in Europe during World War II resulted from racist policies, such as white supremacy, taken to the extreme (e) The Supreme Court's decision in *Plessy* v. *Ferguson* upheld the constitutionality of separate but equal laws. (f) Mob murder was called lynching in the South and vigilante justice in the West.

4. Students should stress that lynching violated the most basic principles of due process.

5. Students should capture some of the practical nature of instruction as well as the creativity of the research done by Carver.

6. Washington's ideas were reactions to the poverty and deep-rooted prejudices he experienced and saw affecting other black Southerners.

7. because DuBois anticipated the civil rights movement of the 1950s and 1960s.

8. DuBois felt that no avenue should be closed to people and that to start at the bottom was to accept white prejudice.

9. application of the law to all races equally

10. Answers should focus on the realization of the promises in the 14th and 15th Amendments.

RESOURCE PAGE 1

QUESTIONS ABOUT THIS RESOURCE PAGE ARE RAISED BY THE TEACHER DURING CLASS DISCUSSION.

RESOURCE PAGE 2

1. because it provides information that they probably did not receive as slaves 2. to inspire and inform readers 3. pride in the achievements of another black American; inspiration to succeed

RESOURCE PAGE 3

1.threats to the constitutional rights of black citizens of Alabama 2. interfere to protect the rights of black citizens 3. crimes against them go unpunished **4.** both documents cite violation of the rights and threat to the lives of black citizens; the petition from Kentucky was sent to Congress; the appeal from black citizens of Alabama was sent to President Grant who then sent it to Congress; probably no action was taken

RESOURCE PAGE 4

1. Singing helped to pass the time and relieve boredom on the trail or at work on the railroad. **2.** People were captivated by the romance of the West and the excitement of the railroad that linked East and West. **3.** "a premature blast went off"; set off explosives to blast through rock

RESOURCE PAGE 5

STUDENTS SHOULD MARK CITIES ON BOTH MAPS. PARAGRAPHS SHOULD NOTE THAT THE GROWTH OF THE RAILROADS PARALLELED AND PROMOTED THE GROWTH OF THESE WESTERN CITIES.

RESOURCE PAGE 6

1. to preserve order and protect the country from the "danger" of Chinese laborers **2.** people opposed to Chinese immigrants **3.** ten years

RESOURCE PAGE 7

1. Wyoming, Colorado, Idaho **2.** 30 states, of which 8 granted women that right in 1919 **3.** the West **4.** These states were younger and more open to equal rights; women worked as hard as men to tame the wilderness.

RESOURCE PAGE 8

1. taught them about the government of their new country **2.** After 1920 women were among those who had the right of suffrage. **3.** Answers will vary.

RESOURCE PAGE 9

1. passionate, angry, dramatic, persuasive, eloquent **2.** Students may be shocked by the number and brutality of lynchings described. **3.** "men who stand in the high esteem of the public" **4.** Possible answer: "What can I do to help your campaign against lynching?"

STUDENT STUDY GUIDE ANSWER KEY

CHAPTER 1
Word Bank 1 Reconstruction; 2. polyglot
Making Inferences 1. E, 2. N, 3. N, 4. S, 5. S, 6. S, 7. S, 8. N.
Primary Source 1.lively, 2. not as important, 3. CE, modern era, 4. discuss

CHAPTER 2 / CHAPTER 3
Word Bank 1.Sewaard's Folly; 2. traitor, 3. black codes, 4. compromise, 5. martial law.
Fact or Opinion 1. O, 2. F 3. O, 4. F, 5. F, 6. O, 7. F, 8. O
Primary Source 1. students, 2. there were young, 3. intelligent or energetic, 4. discuss

CHAPTER 4
Word Bank 1 unalienable, inalienable; 2. states' rights, nullify; 3. civil rights.
Sequence of Events 7, 4, 8, 1, 5, 3, 2, 6
Primary Sources 1. deny, 2. trial, 3. control, 4. fair treatment, 5.-6. discuss

CHAPTER 5
Word Bank 1. integrity 2. illiterate
Drawing Conclusions 1. b, c; 2. a, c; 3. a, c.
Map 1. No. became a separate state in 1862, 2. Tennessee, 3. 1868, 4. Texas, Virginia, Georgia

CHAPTER 6 / CHAPTER 7
Word Bank 1. impeach, 2. high crimes, 3. misdemeanors, 4. balance of power, 5. bigotry, 6. conviction
Making Inferences 1. S, 2. J, 3. S, 4. S, 5. J, 6. S, 7. J.
Primary Sources 1. to impeach, 2. head of Supreme Court, 3. lead, 4. agreement, 5. 67.

CHAPTER 8
Word Bank Have students read sentences aloud. Discuss
Main Idea 1. b, 2. b, 3. a.

CHAPTER 9
Word Bank 1.subverted, 2. patent.
Sequence of Events 4, 2, 3, 8, 6, 7, 5, 1
Primary Sources 1, farms, business; 2. caused terror; 3. Confederates, army has been disbanded

CHAPTER 10
Word Bank 1. lynching, 2. segregated, Jim Crow; 3.poll tax, , 4. share-cropping.
Drawing Conclusions 1. a, b; 2. a, c; 3. a, b.
Primary Sources 1. end of military occupation in South, 2. U.S. government, 3. equality, 4. African Americans.

CHAPTER 11 / CHAPTER 12
Word Bank 1. capital, 2. longhorns, 3. range, 4. depression.
Fact or Opinion 1.O, 2. F, 3. O, 4. F, 5. F, 6. O, 7. F, 8. O.
Map 1. b, 2. a, 3. b, 4. a.

CHAPTER 13
Word Bank 1.visionaries, 2. meridian, 3. subsidy. Read sentences aloud.
Main Idea 1.b, 2. a, 3. b.

Primary Sources 1. it was the fastest travel then, 2. weddings, 3. marry travelers, 4. discuss

CHAPTER 14
Word Bank 1. Pullman Cars, 2. iron horse, 3. emigrant cars, 4. transcontinental.
Making Inferences 1.E, 2. B, 3. E, 4. P, 5. B, 6. P, 7. B, 8. P.

CHAPTER 15
Word Bank 1. Great American Desert, 2. barbed wire, 3. Grange.
Main Idea 1. b, 2. a, 3. b.

CHAPTER 16
Word Bank 1. scythe, 2. sod, 3. reaper, installment buying.
Fact of Opinion 1. F 2. O, 3. O, 4. O 5. F, 6. O, 7. F.
Primary Source 1. center of continent, 2. provide food (life), 3. link between plains and personality, 4. even-tempered.

CHAPTER 17
Word Bank 1. abundance, 2. ceded, 3. extinction, 4. compatible.
Map Discuss notes
Sequence of Events 8, 3, 6, 4, 1, 7, 2, 5.
Primary Sources 1. key to survival, 2. can't eat or wear it, 3. white men, 4. president.

CHAPTER 18
Word Bank 1. rendezvous, 2. reservation, 3. bonanza.
Drawing Conclusions 1. a, b; 2. a, c; 3. a, c.
Map Discuss student's mileage measurements and direction

CHAPTER 19
Word Bank 1. scoundrel, 2. subway, 3. constituent, 4. graft.
Main Idea. 1. c, 2. b, 3. c, 4. b

CHAPTER 20
Word Bank 1. huckster, 2. humbug, 3. prohibition.
Fact or Opinion 1. F, 2. O, 3. O, 4. F, 5. O, 6. F, 7. F, 8. O.
Primary Sources 1. unusual or interesting sights, 2. clowns, 3. bring excitement.

CHAPTER 21
Word Bank 1. exigencies, 2. Gilded Age, 3. sumptuous, 4. apprentice.
Sequence of Events 3, 5, 2, 6, 4, 1, 7.
Primary Sources 1. cutting tool, 2. freezing, 3. no one wants fleas.

CHAPTER 22
Word Bank 1. tenements, 2. emigrate, steerage; 3. immigrate, abysmal.
Making Inferences 1. a, 2. c, 3. b, 4. c, 5. a, 6. c.
Map/Chart 1. decreased, 2. Northern Europe, 3. Canada, 4. about 700,000 people

CHAPTER 23
Word Bank 1. prejudice, 2. racism, 3. anti-Semitic, 4. Know-Nothings.
Drawing Conclusions 1. b, c; 2. a, b; 3. b, c; 4. a, b.
Primary Sources 1. United States, 2. smiled, 3. grew sad, 4. kissed goodbye.

CHAPTER 24 / CHAPTER 25
Word Bank 1. Chinese Exclusion Act, nativism; 2. naturalized citizen, 3. civil law, criminal law; 4. prosecutors, ordinance; 5. defendant, appeal; 6. aliens.

Sequence of Events 3, 5, 4, 6, 1, 8, 2, 7.
Primary Sources Have students read rewrites aloud

CHAPTER 26 / CHAPTER 27
Word Bank 1. veto, 2. suffrage, 3. temperance, benign; 4. justice of the peace.
Making Inferences 1. S, 2. A, 3 A, 4. S, 5. A, 6. S, 7. S, 8. S.

CHAPTER 28
Word Bank 1. beyond the pale, 2. rebbe, shtetl.
Sequence of Events 1. A, 2. B, 3. B, 4. A, 5. A, 6. B, 7. A, 8.B .
Primary Sources 1. foundation, 2. education, 3. earn a living, 4. not free in Russia.

CHAPTER 29 / CHAPTER 30
Word Bank 1. centennial, 2. exports, 3. imports, 4. exposition, 5. stagnating, 6. middle class.
Primary Source 1. easy simple (to describe), 2.extremely, 3. used "giant" (person) metaphor, 4. people were awestruck.

CHAPTER 31
Word Bank 1. filament, 2. dynamos, 3. Morse Code, telegraph.
Fact or Opinion 1. O, 2. F, 3. O, 4. F, 5. F, 6. F, 7. O, 8. O.
Primary Sources 1work at, 2. routine, 3. hard work, 4. perspiration (discuss)

CHAPTER 32
Word Bank 1. segregation, white supremacy; 2. franchise, poll tax; 3. Jim Crow, lynching
Sequence of Events 7, 1, 4, 3, 6, 5, 2
Primary Source 1. black codes, 2. respect for laws, 3. guarantee equality, 4. Confederates.

CHAPTER 33 / CHAPTER 34
Word Bank 1. anarchy, 2. vigilante justice.
Main Idea 1. a, 2. b, 3. b, 4. a.

CHAPTER 35
Word Bank 1.soil-exhausting crops, 2. vocational.
Making Inferences 1. B, 2. A, 3. A, 4. B, 5. B, 6. A, 7. A, 8. A
Primary Source 1. giving in, 2. racist treatment, 3. slaves arrived in the 1600s 4. read restatements aloud.

CHAPTER 36
Word Bank 1. color line, 2. anti-Semitism, 3. civil rights movement.
Making Inferences 1. W , 2. D, 3. D, 4. W, 5. D, 6. D, 7.W, 8. D.
Primary Source 1. born in the United States, 2. beliefs not thoughts, 3.- 4. Discuss.

CHAPTER 37
Word Bank 1. city on a hill, 2. class distinction
Fact or Opinion 1. O, 2. F, 3. O, 4. F, 5. F, 6. F, 7. O.
Primary Source 1. horse, 2. rider. 3. Discuss. 4. Read restatements aloud. Discuss